HARCOURT

SOCIAL Studies

Canada and Latin America

HOUGHTON MIFFLIN HARCOURT
School Publishers

HARCOURT SOCIAL Studies

Canada and Latin America

Series Authors

Dr. Michael J. Berson
Professor
Social Science Education
University of South Florida
Tampa, Florida

Dr. Tyrone C. Howard
Associate Professor
UCLA Graduate School of Education &
    Information Studies
University of California at Los Angeles
Los Angeles, California

Dr. Cinthia Salinas
Assistant Professor
Department of Curriculum and
    Instruction
College of Education
The University of Texas at Austin
Austin, Texas

Content Reviewers

Dr. Christopher J. Kirkey
Director
Center for the Study of Canada
State University of New York College
    at Plattsburgh
Plattsburgh, New York

Dr. Robert B. South
Associate Professor
Department of Geography
University of Cincinnati
Cincinnati, Ohio

Printed in the U.S.A.

ISBN-13: 978-0-15-385889-5
ISBN-10: 0-15-385889-3

2 3 4 5 6 7 8 9 10 0868 18 17 16 15 14 13 12 11 10

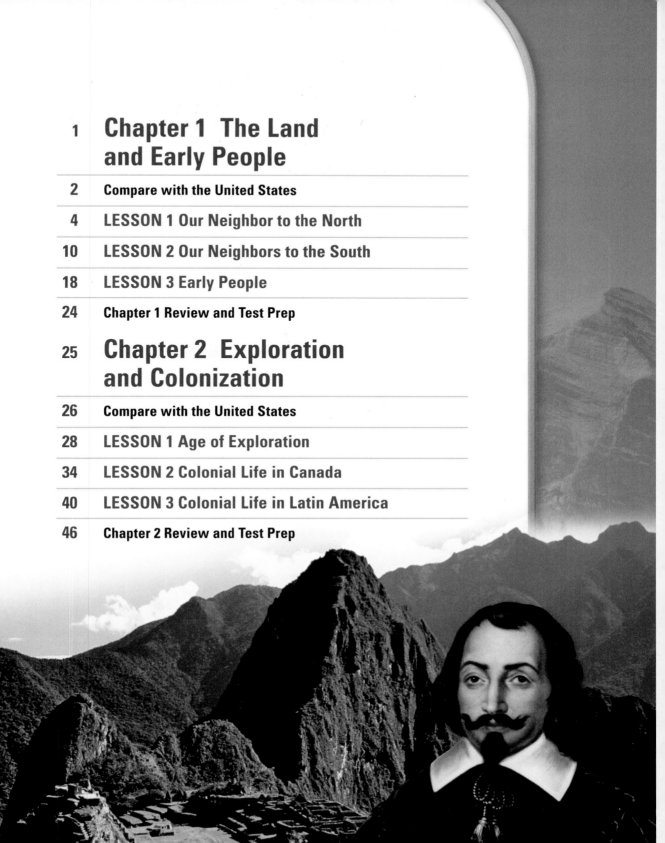

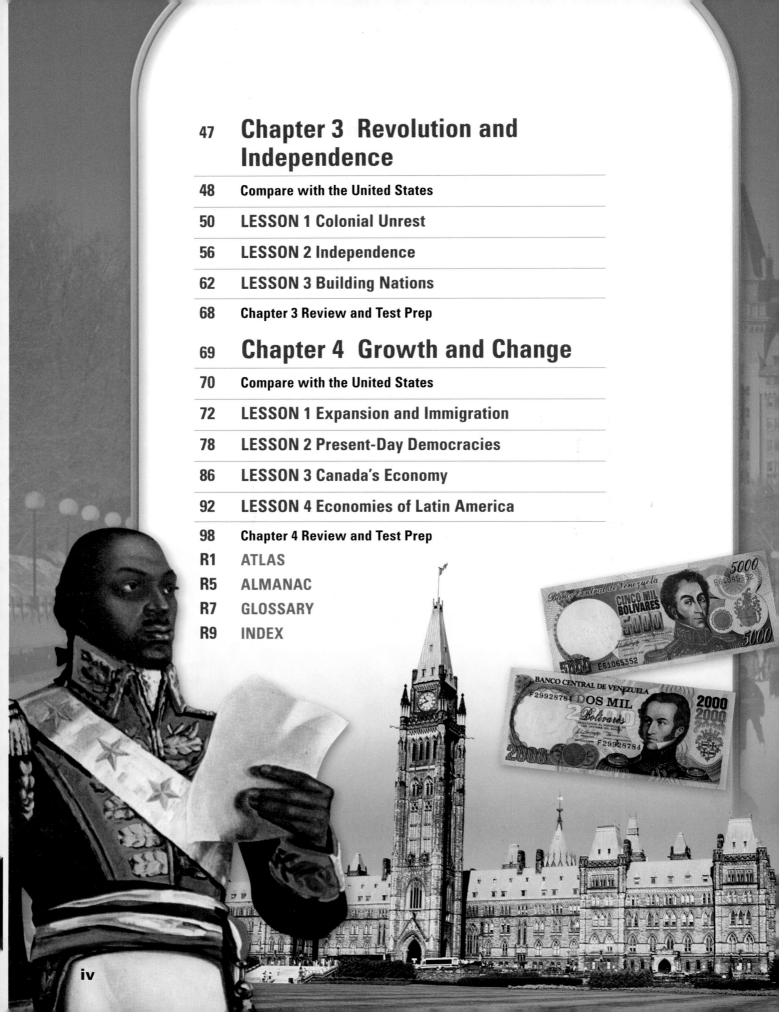

The Land and Early People

▶ CHICHÉN ITZÁ,
YUCATÁN, MEXICO

LESSON 1
Our Neighbor
to the North

LESSON 2
Our Neighbors
to the South

LESSON 3
Early People

Time

About 12,000 years ago
Hunters migrate into Canada

▶ EARLY PEOPLE HUNT WOOLLY MAMMOTHS

About 5,000 years ago
Early Native Americans
begin planting crops

About 1,000 years ago
The Navajo move to
the desert Southwest

About 800 years ago
More than 30,000
people live in Cahokia

5,000 years ago

Present

About 4,000 years ago
Inuit migrate across
northern Canada

About 3,500 years ago Olmec
civilization begins to grow

About 800 years ago Aztec
civilization develops empire

Our Neighbor to the North

WHAT TO KNOW
How are the geography and the climate of Canada different from one region to another?

VOCABULARY
glacier p. 6
timberline p. 6
tundra p. 6
permafrost p. 6
fjord p. 7
muskeg p. 7
cordillera p. 8
tide p. 8

PLACES
Hudson Bay
St. Lawrence River
Mackenzie River
Rocky Mountains
Coast Mountains
Appalachian Mountains
Newfoundland
Nova Scotia
Bay of Fundy

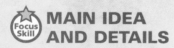

MAIN IDEA AND DETAILS

Main Idea

Details

YOU ARE THERE It's a freezing day in northeastern Canada. You are in your kayak. As you paddle, you think about how your ancestors struggled to survive in this cold region. They used sealskin to make their kayaks. They carved fishing spears from walrus tusks. They lined their coats with caribou fur. You admire the way they made full use of their limited resources. It is an important part of the way of life passed down by the people of northeastern Canada.

❯ BAFFIN ISLAND is the largest island in Canada's Arctic Islands region.

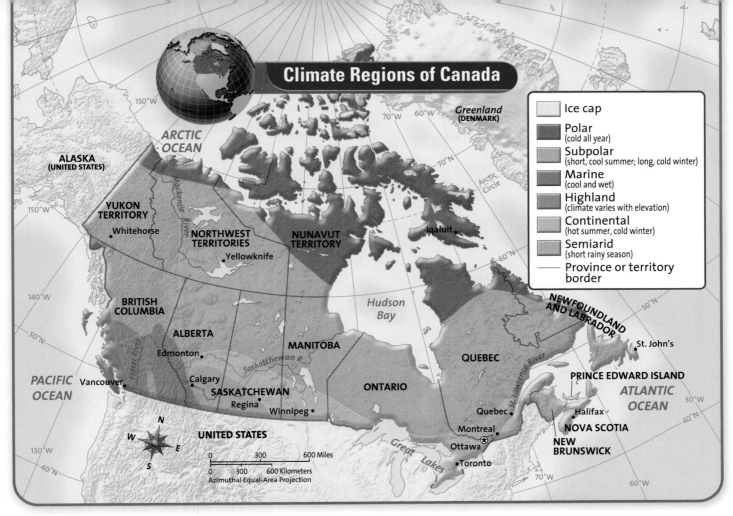

Climate Regions of Canada

Ice cap

Polar (cold all year)

Subpolar (short, cool summer; long, cold winter)

Marine (cool and wet)

Highland (climate varies with elevation)

Continental (hot summer, cold winter)

Semiarid (short rainy season)

— Province or territory border

MAP SKILL **REGIONS** Canada has ten provinces and three territories, instead of states. What climate regions can be found in Alberta province?

A Vast Land

Canada is the second-largest country in the world, behind Russia. It covers most of the northern part of mainland North America. This large country stretches from the Pacific Ocean in the west to the Atlantic Ocean in the east. It shares its long southern border with the United States. From there, Canada extends north to the Arctic Ocean, almost to the North Pole.

Canada's Climate

Canada is larger in size than the United States. Yet its population is only about as large as that of the state of California. Because of the harsh climate in the north, most of Canada's 33.2 million people live within 100 miles of the United States border.

Canada's climate is influenced by its high latitude, or distance from the equator. The polar areas that lie north of the Arctic Circle, at 66° N, receive less heat from the sun than areas to the south. As a result, these areas have cold weather all year round. Southern Canada enjoys a short, warm summer season.

READING CHECK ☼**MAIN IDEA AND DETAILS**
Why do so few people live in northern Canada?

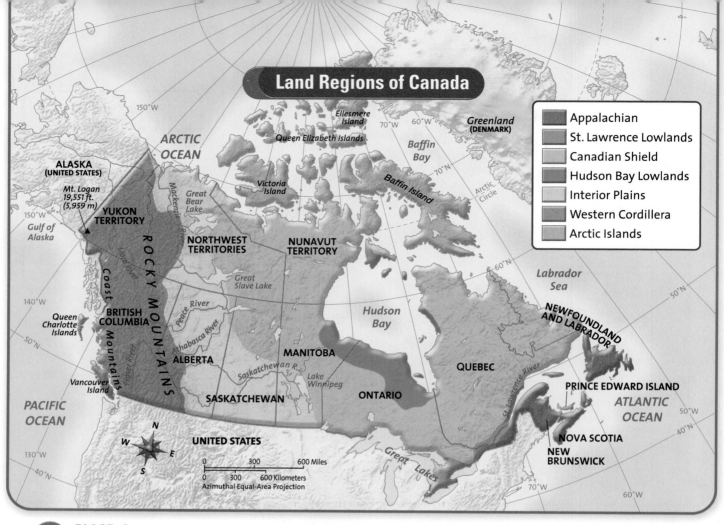

Land Regions of Canada

Legend:
- Appalachian
- St. Lawrence Lowlands
- Canadian Shield
- Hudson Bay Lowlands
- Interior Plains
- Western Cordillera
- Arctic Islands

MAP SKILL PLACE Geographers divide Canada into seven land regions. What two mountain ranges can be found in the Western Cordillera region?

Canada's Land Regions

All large areas have a variety of landforms. The country of Canada has seven different land regions.

The Canadian Shield

The largest region is the Canadian Shield. This rocky area covers almost half the country.

About 12,000 years ago, most of Canada was covered by glaciers (GLAY•sherz). A **glacier** is a large ice mass that moves slowly across land. As the glaciers shifted back and forth, they stripped away much of the Canadian Shield's soil. They wore down its mountains into low hills. They also carved out lakes, rivers, and valleys.

Today, evergreen forests grow in the rocky soil of the southern Canadian Shield. The forests of the Canadian Shield stop at the **timberline**, or tree line. North of the timberline, the climate is too cold for trees to grow. That is why the northern part of the Canadian Shield is covered by a **tundra**, or treeless plain. Canada's tundra has only a thin layer of frozen soil called **permafrost**.

The Arctic Islands

The tundra extends north of the Canadian Shield into the Arctic Islands region. This region is made up of 12 large islands and thousands of smaller ones. Many of the Arctic islands are surrounded by **fjords** (fee•AWRDZ), or narrow inlets of sea with steep cliffs.

The Hudson Bay Lowlands

The country of Canada has many rivers and streams. The ones located south of **Hudson Bay** do not drain well. Because of this, the Hudson Bay Lowlands region is covered with boggy swamplands called **muskegs** (MUHS•kegz).

St. Lawrence Lowlands

Canada's richest farmland is found in the St. Lawrence Lowlands region. This fertile region is named after Canada's third-longest river. The **St. Lawrence River** stretches 740 miles along Canada's southeastern border. It connects the Atlantic Ocean and the Great Lakes.

In 1959, Canada and the United States built a series of locks and canals on the St. Lawrence River. Now, the St. Lawrence Seaway's canals allow ships to pass around parts of the river that are too shallow.

The Interior Plains

As in the St. Lawrence Lowlands, fertile farmland makes up the southern part of Canada's Interior Plains region. The flat and grassy landscape of the southern Interior Plains is very much like the plains of the United States. In the northwestern corner of the Interior Plains are evergreen forests and Canada's longest river, the **Mackenzie River**.

▶ Ships use the St. Lawrence River (right) to carry goods between the Atlantic Ocean and Canada's Interior Plains region (below).

The Western Cordillera

West of the Interior Plains is the Western Cordillera region. A **cordillera** (kawr•duhl•YAIR•uh) is a system of parallel mountain ranges.

The **Rocky Mountains** run along the eastern edge of the Western Cordillera region. The **Coast Mountains** run along the western edge. The tallest mountain in the Western Cordillera is Mount Logan, at 19,551 feet. Between the ranges are smaller mountains, as well as plateaus and valleys.

The Appalachian Region

Mountains can also be found in the eastern part of Canada. Canada's Appalachian region is named after the **Appalachian Mountains.** Over thousands of years, erosion has worn away parts of these very old mountains.

Between the mountains and hills in the region lies fertile land.

Several islands are found alongside Canada's eastern coast. The largest of these is the island of **Newfoundland**.

South of Newfoundland is the land of **Nova Scotia**. The **Bay of Fundy** on Nova Scotia's southern edge has some of the world's highest tides. A **tide** is the regular rise and fall of the ocean and bodies of water connected to it.

At certain times of the year, the tides in the Bay of Fundy rise more than 50 feet. The powerful tides have carved enormous rock towers from the cliffs that line the bay. The tides also cause the St. John River to flow upriver, creating a natural feature known as the Reversing Falls.

READING CHECK ◕**MAIN IDEA AND DETAILS**
What are the seven land regions of Canada?

FAST FACT

Banff National Park in the Canadian Rocky Mountains became Canada's first national park in 1885.

Canada's Resources

Canada's great wealth of natural resources helps make up for its small amounts of fertile land. Those natural resources are timber, oil, natural gas, coal, minerals, and animals, including fish.

The thick forests of the Western Cordillera and the Canadian Shield regions supply the country's timber industry. Those regions also contain iron, zinc, nickel, copper, uranium, gold, silver, and other metals.

In 1947, oil and natural gas were discovered in Canada's Interior Plains region. Oil and natural gas are also found near the Atlantic and Arctic coasts.

Canada's lakes and river systems provide a rich environment for caribou, moose, deer, foxes, and beaver. These animals are important to the country's meat, leather,

▶ **APPALACHIAN REGION** Nova Scotia is one of many fishing areas in the Appalachian region.

and fur industries. The Atlantic and Pacific Oceans offer rich harvests of fish. Hydroelectric plants also use the country's water resources to produce electricity.

READING CHECK ☼**MAIN IDEA AND DETAILS**
What are some of Canada's most important natural resources?

REVIEW

1. **WHAT TO KNOW** How are the geography and the climate of Canada different from one region to another?

2. **VOCABULARY** Write a sentence that describes the **tundra**.

3. **HISTORY** How did Canada and the United States improve the St. Lawrence River for shipping?

4. **GEOGRAPHY** How are the climates north and south of the timberline in the Canadian Shield different?

5. **CRITICAL THINKING** Where in Canada is the geography most like where you live?

6. 🖌 **MAKE A BROCHURE** Write and illustrate a travel brochure that invites visitors to see Canada's beauty.

Lesson 2

Our Neighbors to the South

WHAT TO KNOW

How are the geography and the climate of Latin America different from one part to another?

VOCABULARY

isthmus p. 12

sierra p. 13

peninsula p. 13

Ring of Fire p. 14

trade winds p. 15

rain forest p. 16

tributary p. 16

altiplano p. 17

PLACES

Isthmus of Tehuantepec

Plateau of Mexico

Mexico City

Sierra Madre Occidental

Sierra Madre Oriental

Baja California

Yucatán Peninsula

Patagonia

Llanos

Pampas

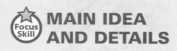

MAIN IDEA AND DETAILS

Main Idea

Details

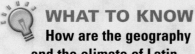 **YOU ARE THERE** It's a hot, clear day in Costa Rica, where you're visiting relatives. As you eat lunch outside, you look up and see a puff of smoke coming out of the volcano across the valley. "Don't worry," your aunt assures you. "It happens all the time." Your cousin adds, "It's farther away than you think." Then she calmly returns to eating her dessert.

▶ THE ARENAL VOLCANO in Costa Rica

Latin America

Latin America is an enormous region. It stretches from the northern edge of Mexico in North America to the southern tip of South America. The region contains 33 countries and 13 territories. It is larger than the United States and Canada together.

Latin America includes Mexico, Central America, the Caribbean islands, and South America. Central America is made up of the seven North American countries south of Mexico.

Because Latin America is so large, its geography varies from one part of the region to another. Mountains, volcanoes, coral islands, forests, and deserts can all be found in Latin America.

The Tropics

Much of Latin America lies in the tropical climate region. This is the region that circles Earth close to the equator. The sun shines directly overhead in the tropics. For this reason, the climate is warm year-round.

Even in the tropics, climates change. In high places, temperatures get colder as elevation increases. During

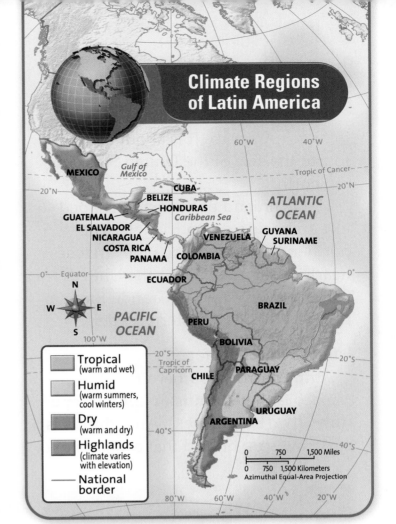

Climate Regions of Latin America

MAP SKILL **REGIONS** Which of Latin America's climate regions can be found in Guatemala?

rainy seasons, some lowland areas are drenched with as much as 100 inches of rain. Palm trees, tropical fruits, and a variety of crops grow well in Latin America's warm, rainy climates.

READING CHECK ⊙**MAIN IDEA AND DETAILS**
What causes warm climates in Latin America?

Mexico

Mexico is the third-largest country in North America. It is about one-fourth the size of the United States to the north.

The mainland of Mexico is shaped like an upside-down triangle. The northern base of the triangle stretches nearly 2,000 miles along the United States border. The Rio Grande forms much of the northeastern border.

Isthmus of Tehuantepec

At the narrow southern tip of Mexico is the **Isthmus of Tehuantepec** (tuh•HWAHN•tuh•pek). An **isthmus** is a narrow strip of land that connects two larger areas of land. At the Isthmus of Tehuantepec, the distance between the Pacific Ocean and the Gulf of Mexico is only about 137 miles.

Plateau of Mexico

Mexico is one of the world's most densely populated countries. More than 109 million people live in Mexico. In contrast, only 33.2 million live in Canada, which is four times larger in area than Mexico.

Most of Mexico's people live in the high central **Plateau of Mexico**. This plateau rises to about 8,000 feet above sea level. **Mexico City** is the capital of Mexico. It is located on the Plateau of Mexico.

▶ **MEXICO CITY** (below) is located on the Plateau of Mexico. The desert region north of the Plateau of Mexico stretches to the United States border at the Rio Grande (left).

Deserts, Mountains, and Volcanoes

The Plateau of Mexico is surrounded by low deserts in the north and by mountain ranges in the east and west. The **Sierra Madre Occidental** runs along the west coast. The **Sierra Madre Oriental** is on the east. A **sierra** is any rugged chain of mountains.

Located along the southern end of the Plateau of Mexico is a chain of volcanoes. Many are active, or may erupt in the future. These volcanoes are formed by the movement of Earth's surface. This movement also causes earthquakes.

The Plateau of Mexico has many earthquakes. Some destroy homes and injure or kill people.

Peninsulas

Two **peninsulas**, or land almost completely surrounded by water, jut out from the northwestern and southeastern corners of Mexico. The thinly populated peninsula in the northwestern corner is called **Baja** (BAH•hah) **California**, or Lower California. It is separated from Mexico's mainland by the Gulf of California.

The **Yucatán Peninsula** extends into the Gulf of Mexico. It shares its southern border with Belize (buh•LEEZ) and Guatemala (gwah•tay•MAH•lah) in Central America.

READING CHECK ☼**MAIN IDEA AND DETAILS**
How would you describe the size and population of Mexico?

▶ **HUMAN-ENVIRONMENT INTERACTIONS** The locks on the Panama Canal raise and lower the water level so that ships can pass to the next part of the canal.

Central America

Central America is made up of seven countries—Belize, Costa Rica, El Salvador, Guatemala, Honduras, Nicaragua (nee•kah•RAH•gwah), and Panama. The combined land of the seven countries covers an area smaller than that of the state of Texas.

To the west of Central America lies the Pacific Ocean. To the east is the Caribbean Sea.

In 1914, the United States completed work on the Panama Canal. The canal is located in the southern part of Central America in the country of Panama. It allows ships to travel between the Pacific Ocean and the Caribbean Sea. Today, the canal is controlled by the government of Panama.

The Ring of Fire

Most Central American countries are mountainous. Only along the coasts are there lowlands. The land remains low for a short distance before rising.

Central America's mountains were formed by volcanoes. In fact, the region's mountains are part of the **Ring of Fire**. This term refers to a circle of volcanoes along the edges of the Pacific Ocean.

Central America could be called the Land of Volcanoes. The west coast of Nicaragua alone has about 40 active volcanoes. Ash from volcanoes helps keep the soil of the Central American highlands fertile.

READING CHECK ŏ**MAIN IDEA AND DETAILS**
What is the main kind of landform found in Central America?

The Caribbean Islands

The Caribbean islands are located between Florida and Venezuela in South America. They stretch 2,000 miles across the Caribbean Sea.

Some of these islands were formed by volcanic eruptions. Others were made from the buildup of sand, limestone, and coral over a long time. Coral is a hard, bony substance made up of the skeletons of tiny sea animals.

Trade Winds

The Caribbean islands can be divided into three groups—the Greater Antilles, the Lesser Antilles, and the Bahamas. Cuba, Hispaniola (ees•pah•NYOH•lah), Jamaica, and Puerto Rico are in the Greater Antilles.

The Lesser Antilles are southeast of Puerto Rico. They are divided into two chains of islands—the Windward Islands and the Leeward Islands.

The Windward Islands are in the path of the trade winds. The Leeward Islands are not in the path of the trade winds. **Trade winds** blow northeast and southeast from the equator.

The trade winds help produce mild weather. However, they also place the Caribbean in the path of hurricanes during the summer.

Like most coral islands, the Bahamas are low-lying islands with little vegetation. Unfortunately, these islands have little fertile soil. Most people in the Bahamas live on Grand Bahama and New Providence islands.

READING CHECK ⓈMAIN IDEA AND DETAILS
What are the three groups of islands in the Caribbean region?

▶ **LESSER ANTILLES** Palm trees line Harrismith Beach on the island nation of Barbados in the Lesser Antilles.

Layers of the Rain Forest

ILLUSTRATION Each layer of the rain forest is home to many different plants and animals. What plants and animals do you see in this illustration?

Emergent Layer

Canopy Layer

Understory Layer

Forest Floor

South America

South America is known for its remarkable physical features. The land area covered by South America's 13 countries is more than twice the size of the United States. The region's Andes Mountains form the world's longest mountain range. The long and winding Amazon River is surrounded by the world's largest rain forest. A **rain forest** is a woodland that gets a large amount of rainfall. Rain forests have thick vegetation and tall trees that block the sunlight.

The Amazon River

The Amazon River is the second-longest river in the world. It winds nearly 4,000 miles from the foot of the Andes Mountains to its mouth at the Atlantic Ocean. Along the way, the Amazon collects water from more than 1,000 tributaries (TRIB•yoo•tair•eez). A **tributary** is a stream or river that flows into a larger stream or river.

One-fifth of the world's supply of fresh water flows through the Amazon River. One-third of the world's plants and animal species live in the surrounding Amazon rain forest.

The Atacama Desert

The Atacama (ah•tah•KAH•mah) Desert, on the west coast of Chile, is one of the world's driest areas. **Patagonia**, a dry area east of the Andes, gets only about 8 inches of rainfall each year. Some areas of the Atacama get no rainfall at all.

> **THE ANDES MOUNTAINS** cross through all or part of Argentina, Colombia, Ecuador, Peru, Bolivia, Venezuela, and Chile.

The Andes Mountains

The Andes Mountains run along 4,500 miles of South America's west coast. Between the mountain ranges of Peru and Bolivia is an **altiplano** (al•tih•PLAH•noh), or high plain. Ranchers on the altiplano raise llamas, alpacas, and sheep.

The South American Plains

The South American plains cover a large part of South America. The tropical plains in Venezuela and south western Colombia are called the **Llanos** (yah•nohs). The **Pampas** (pam•puhs) is a grassy plains region in Argentina.

The Pampas region is known for its many sheep and cattle ranches.

The North Coast

North of the Amazon River are the Guiana Highlands. The countries of Colombia, Venezuela, Guyana, and Suriname are all located here, as is French Guiana, a French territory. Farm products from the region include sugar, coffee, rice, and bananas. Much of Venezuela's wealth comes from its oil industry.

READING CHECK Ŏ**MAIN IDEA AND DETAILS**
What are some of the most important physical features of South America?

REVIEW

1. **WHAT TO KNOW** How are the geography and the climate of Latin America different from one part to another?

2. **VOCABULARY** Write a sentence about Central America's geography that uses the term **Ring of Fire**.

3. **HISTORY** Who built the Panama Canal, and who controls it now?

4. **GEOGRAPHY** What different land regions surround the central plateau of Mexico?

5. **CRITICAL THINKING** How is the geography of Latin America like that of the United States? How is it different?

6. **WRITE A LETTER** Imagine that you have just come back from a trip through two neighboring countries in Latin America. Write a letter to a friend telling about the trip. Describe the similarities and differences between the lands, climates, plants, and animals.

Lesson 3

about 12,000 years ago
Hunters migrate into Canada

about 7,000 years ago
Early peoples are farming in Mexico

about 3,500 years ago
Olmec civilization begins to grow

WHAT TO KNOW
Who were the early people in Canada and Latin America?

VOCABULARY
First Nations p. 19
maize p. 20
agriculture p. 20
culture p. 21
civilization p. 22
empire p. 23

PLACES
Tenochtitlán
Monte Verde
Caral
Cuzco

MAIN IDEA AND DETAILS

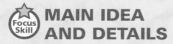

Early People

YOU ARE THERE

"Hurry along, please!" Your father urges you to keep up with him as he weaves through the crowded Aztec market in the city of **Tenochtitlán** (tay•nohch•teet•LAHN). You are carrying corn, which was grown on your farm, to trade for cloth. People are trading everything from painted cloth and pottery to gold jewelry and unusual feathers. You can't stop staring at a colorful mask decorated with precious stones.

▶ AZTEC MARKET at Tenochtitlán

Early Migration

The earliest people to live in the Americas probably migrated from Asia more than 12,000 years ago. During the last Ice Age, the level of the oceans dropped greatly. This created a land bridge connecting Asia and North America.

Migrating into Canada

Over many years, people may have slowly traveled over the land bridge into North America. Some of these people migrated to what is today southern Canada. They were the ancestors of Canada's **First Nations**. Most Native Canadians today are members of the First Nations. One exception is the Inuit (IN•yoo•it) people of northern Canada.

Migrating South

It is not clear how early people arrived on the continent of South America. Some may have migrated

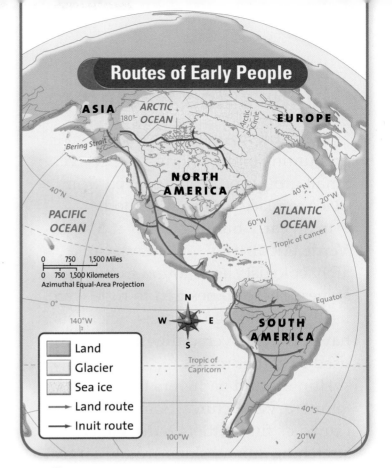

Routes of Early People

0 750 1,500 Miles
0 750 1,500 Kilometers
Azimuthal Equal-Area Projection

Land
Glacier
Sea ice
→ Land route
→ Inuit route

MAP SKILL **MOVEMENT** What two routes did early people take into Canada?

on foot from the north. Others may have traveled by boat.

READING CHECK ⏺**MAIN IDEA AND DETAILS**
What continent did the early people of the Americas probably migrate from?

Hunters and Gatherers

The earliest Americans depended on hunting and gathering to survive. Small groups of people moved from place to place in search of food.

In an early hunting camp at **Monte Verde** (MOHN•tay VAIR•day), Chile, archaeologists have found throwing stones. These stones tied to rope were used to hunt large animals. Scientists have also uncovered digging sticks, used to gather roots.

Hunters and gatherers lived in temporary structures. Some of Canada's first settlers built tents by stretching animal skins around large animal tusks. Early people on Bolivia's altiplano lived in lean-to shelters. Arawak (AIR•uh•wahk) people in the Caribbean slept in swinging rope beds.

Early Farmers

By 7,000 years ago, early people in central Mexico were growing crops of beans, squash, and **maize**, or corn. **Agriculture**, or farming, allowed people to settle in one place and build permanent villages. Some of these grew into cities. The oldest known city in the Americas has been found near **Caral**, Peru. It dates back to 2700 B.C.

READING CHECK ⭕**MAIN IDEA AND DETAILS**
How did farming change the lives of early people?

⟩ **EARLY HUNTERS AND GATHERERS** in Monte Verde, Chile

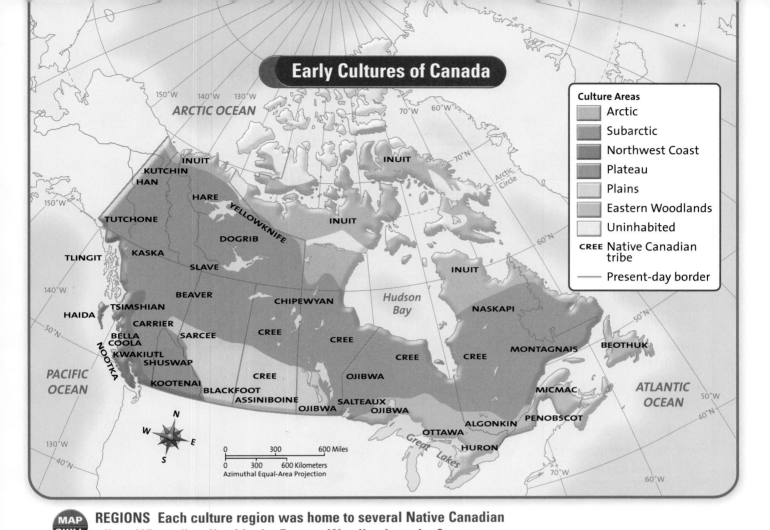

Early Cultures of Canada

Culture Areas
- Arctic
- Subarctic
- Northwest Coast
- Plateau
- Plains
- Eastern Woodlands
- Uninhabited
- CREE Native Canadian tribe
- — Present-day border

MAP SKILL **REGIONS** Each culture region was home to several Native Canadian tribes. What tribes lived in the Eastern Woodlands region?

Early Canadians

Canada's early people lived in six regions. Each region developed a different culture based partly on its natural resources. A **culture** is a way of life shared by a group.

Eastern Woodlands Culture

The Eastern Woodlands people lived in what is now southeastern Canada. They built longhouses and wigwams out of timber. Their main crops were corn, beans, and squash. They traveled in canoes made from the bark of birch trees.

Arctic Culture

The early Inuit often traveled very long distances for food, using kayaks as well as sleds pulled by dogs. They built temporary ice huts called igloos (IH•glooz). Their permanent huts were made of sod and stones.

Subarctic Culture

People of the Subarctic culture lived in the thick forests of the northern Canadian Shield. They depended on the animals they hunted to get food, clothing, and shelter. They lived in wigwams and built wooden canoes and sleds called toboggans (tuh•BAH•guhnz).

Early Cultures of Latin America

Culture Areas
- California
- Southwest
- Middle America
- Caribbean
- Andes
- Tropical Forest
- Marginal

Civilizations
- Aztec
- Maya
- Inca

- ● Major settlement
- OLMEC Native American tribe
- — Present-day border

MAP SKILL **REGIONS** Many different culture groups lived in Latin America. What culture groups lived in what is today Mexico?

Northwest Coast Culture

Some peoples of the Northwest Coast culture made large rectangular houses and dugout canoes from wood. Using the canoes, they fished for salmon and hunted whales.

Plains and Plateau Cultures

Members of the Plains culture hunted large buffalo herds. They used the buffalo skins to make clothing and tents called **tepees** (TEE·peez).

People of the Plateau culture depended on deer and salmon. They lived in round earthen houses.

READING CHECK Ŏ**MAIN IDEA AND DETAILS**
What were Canada's six early culture groups?

Early Civilizations

The first civilization to form in the Americas began about 3,500 years ago. A **civilization** is a group with its own ways of life, religion, and learning.

The Olmec Civilization

The Olmec civilization lasted from about 1500 B.C. to A.D. 300. In the northern part of Mexico's Isthmus of Tehuantepec, the Olmec built cities with pyramids, temples, and plazas. They developed their own calendar. They also carved giant stone heads in honor of their rulers.

The Mayan Civilization

Between A.D. 300 and A.D. 900, the Mayan civilization flourished. The Maya ruled much of what are now southern Mexico, Guatemala, and Belize.

The Maya are remembered for their writing system, their cities, and their flat-topped pyramids. The Maya's writing system allowed them to record their history. They built more than 100 stone cities.

The Aztec Empire

About A.D. 1200, the people of the Aztec civilization began to settle Mexico's central plateau. The Aztecs built their capital city of Tenochtitlán where Mexico City is today.

In time, the Aztecs came to control central and southern Mexico. Their civilization covered about 200,000 square miles. It had more than 5 million people. In this way, the Aztecs formed one of the earliest empires in the Americas. An **empire** is a collection of lands ruled by the nation that won control of them.

▶ **INCA EMPIRE** Ruins of the Inca city of Machu Picchu still stand in the Andes Mountains of Peru.

The Inca Empire

Between A.D. 1438 and A.D. 1533, the Inca formed an even larger empire on the western coast of South America. From their capital city of **Cuzco** (COO•skoh), they ruled more than 12 million people. To connect the parts of their empire, the Inca built two major road systems.

READING CHECK ◔ MAIN IDEA AND DETAILS
What are four civilizations that developed in Latin America?

REVIEW

1. **WHAT TO KNOW** Who were the early people in Canada and Latin America?

2. **VOCABULARY** Use the word **civilization** in a sentence about the Olmec.

3. **ECONOMICS** How did agriculture change the way people lived?

4. **CULTURE** How did Canada's early people use the trees from their forests?

5. **CRITICAL THINKING** Why do you think Canada had so many different native cultures?

6. **DRAW A MAP** Draw a map showing the locations of the Aztec and Inca Empires. Clearly draw the borders and label the capital city of each empire.

Review and Test Prep

 Vocabulary

Identify the term from the word bank that correctly matches each definition.

1. a high plain

2. a thin layer of frozen soil

3. lands ruled by the nation that conquered them

4. a circle of volcanoes around the edges of the Pacific Ocean

5. a line north of which no trees can grow

6. land that is almost completely surrounded by water

7. a rugged chain of mountains

8. a boggy swampland

Word Bank

timberline p. 6	**peninsula** p. 13
permafrost p. 6	**Ring of Fire** p. 14
muskeg p. 7	**altiplano** p. 17
sierra p. 13	**empire** p. 23

 Facts and Main Ideas

Answer these questions.

9. What are some of Canada's most valuable natural resources?

10. What South American desert is one of the world's driest areas?

11. What is the oldest-known city in the Americas?

12. What river supplies one-fifth of the world's fresh water?

Write the letter of the best choice.

13. Canada's richest farmland is located in
 A the St. Lawrence Lowlands
 B the Appalachian region
 C the Canadian Shield
 D the Western Cordillera

14. How are volcanoes formed?
 A the action of the tides
 B the movement of Earth's surface
 C the carving out of the land by glaciers
 D the force of the trade winds

15. Which civilization was the earliest?
 A Inca
 B Olmec
 C Aztec
 D Maya

Critical Thinking

16. Why does the Canadian Shield not have any high mountains?

17. Why do you think that many different kinds of plants grow in the Amazon rain forest?

18. Why did the Inuit build their shelters of different materials from those used by other native cultures in Canada?

writing

Write an Informative Report
Do some research to find out how the population of Mexico City has changed over the past 50 years. Compare this to how the population of the whole country of Mexico has changed. Write an informational report about your findings.

Exploration and Colonization

CHAPTER 2

QUEBEC CITY,
QUEBEC, CANADA

LESSON 1
Age of Exploration

LESSON 2
Colonial Life in Canada

LESSON 3
Colonial Life
in Latin America

Time

• United States

1513 Juan Ponce de León reaches Florida

1585 The first colonists arrive at Roanoke

Compare with the United States

1450

1550

• Canada

1497 John Cabot reaches Newfoundland and Labrador

1534 Jacques Cartier explores the St. Lawrence River

• Latin America

1492 Christopher Columbus claims land in the Americas for Spain

1500 Pedro Cabral claims land in Brazil for Portugal

COLONISTS IN NEW YORK CITY

1619 The first Africans arrive in Virginia

1620 English Pilgrims settle Plymouth Colony

1681 William Penn founds Pennsylvania Colony

1720s The Great Awakening begins in the Middle Colonies

1650

1750

1608 Samuel de Champlain starts settlement at Quebec

1610 Henry Hudson sails into Hudson Bay and claims it for the English

1749 Halifax becomes the capital of Nova Scotia

1531 Francisco Pizarro conquers the Inca Empire

1654 The Dutch in northern Brazil surrender land to the Portuguese

Time

1450   1750

1492
Columbus lands in
San Salvador

1519
Conquistadors land
in Mexico

1534
Cartier explores
Canada

WHAT TO KNOW
Why did Europeans explore Canada and Latin America, and what did they find?

VOCABULARY
navigation p. 29
line of demarcation p. 30
conquistador p. 30
Northwest Passage p. 32

PEOPLE
Motecuhzoma
Christopher Columbus
Pedro Cabral
Hernando Cortés
Malintzin
Francisco Pizarro
Atahuallpa
John Cabot
Henry Hudson
Jacques Cartier

PLACES
Tenochtitlán
Newfoundland and
    Labrador
San Salvador
Quebec

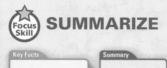

SUMMARIZE

Key Facts	Summary

Age of Exploration

YOU ARE THERE
Strange people in metal suits are marching toward your hometown of **Tenochtitlán,** the Aztec capital. They are riding large animals and carrying powerful weapons.
You watch as Emperor **Motecuhzoma** (moh•tay•kwah•SOH•mah) puts a necklace around the neck of one of the strangers. You wonder if the stranger could be a god. Has he come to rule the empire?

▶ **EMPEROR MOTECUHZOMA** meets a Spanish explorer.

▶ **THE VIKINGS** built sod huts like these on the island of Newfoundland.

Sailing to the West

A group of Vikings landed on the northeastern coast of present-day Canada in about A.D. 1000. The Vikings were from Norway. They sailed from Greenland to what is now **Newfoundland and Labrador.** After a few years, they sailed home. Europeans did not return to the Americas for another 500 years.

Sea Routes to Asia

In the 1400s, European traders had a problem. They needed to find faster and safer sea routes to trade centers in Asia. Explorers from Portugal reached India by sailing around Africa. Other explorers believed that they could sail directly west from Europe to Asia. They did not realize that North America and South America lay in between.

New Ships and New Tools

European explorers learned to sail a new kind of ship called a caravel. A caravel was faster and lighter than other ships. This meant that it could travel across rough oceans. It could also carry more cargo.

In addition, explorers improved their navigation skills. **Navigation** is the science of planning and following a route. Explorers used tools such as the compass and astrolabe. They also made more-accurate maps.

READING CHECK ⏱ **SUMMARIZE**
Why did Europeans sail west to North America?

Exploring Latin America

In August 1492, **Christopher Columbus** left the port of Palos, Spain, with three caravels. He was an Italian explorer sailing for the king of Spain. Columbus and his crew reached the Caribbean island of **San Salvador** two months later. They were greeted by the native Taino people. Columbus called them Indians. He thought he had reached India, in Asia.

The Line of Demarcation

Columbus claimed the island for Spain. He did not find spices or silk. He did take back gold and new kinds of plants back to Spain. Most of Europe's kings then wanted to send explorers across the Atlantic.

In 1493, Portugal challenged Spain's land claims. The Pope settled the disagreement. On a map, he drew a **line of demarcation**, or a line that marks a boundary. Spain could claim land west of the imaginary line. Portugal could claim land east of it. **Pedro Cabral** (kah•BRAHL) claimed what is now Brazil for Portugal in 1500.

Conquistadors

The Spanish sent explorers called conquistadors (kahn•KEES•tuh•dawrz), or "conquerors," to Latin America. The **conquistadors** claimed land for Spain. They also searched for gold and other treasures.

Cortés

One of the first conquistadors was **Hernando Cortés** (air•NAHN•doh kawr•TES). In 1519, Cortés landed on

▶ **EXPLORERS** used tools such as this astrolabe (right) to navigate across the Atlantic Ocean in caravels (below).

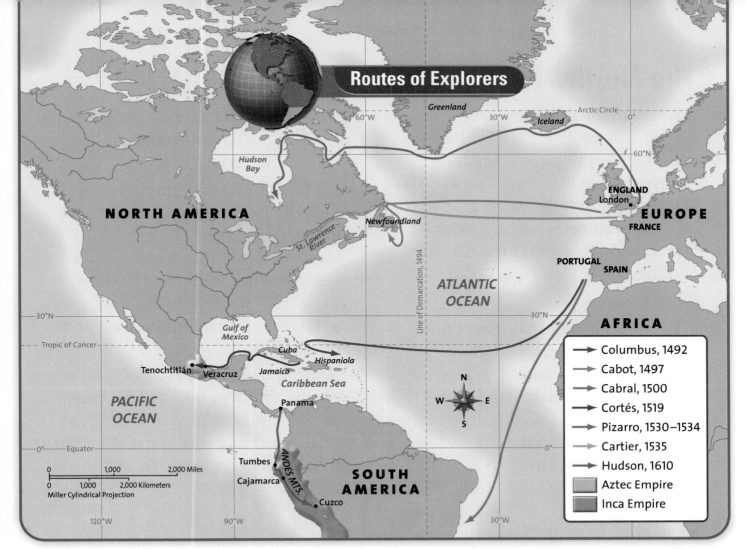

Routes of Explorers

NORTH AMERICA

Hudson Bay

Greenland

Iceland

Arctic Circle

ENGLAND
London

EUROPE
FRANCE

PORTUGAL
SPAIN

Newfoundland

St. Lawrence River

Line of Demarcation, 1494

ATLANTIC
OCEAN

AFRICA

Gulf of
Mexico

Cuba

Hispaniola

Tenochtitlán   Veracruz   Jamaica

Caribbean Sea

N
W   E
S

PACIFIC
OCEAN

Panama

Tumbes

Cajamarca

ANDES MTS.

SOUTH
AMERICA

Cuzco

Tropic of Cancer

30°N

Equator

0   1,000   2,000 Miles
0   1,000   2,000 Kilometers
Miller Cylindrical Projection

120°W   90°W   30°W

→ Columbus, 1492
→ Cabot, 1497
→ Cabral, 1500
→ Cortés, 1519
→ Pizarro, 1530–1534
→ Cartier, 1535
→ Hudson, 1610
   Aztec Empire
   Inca Empire

MAP SKILL **MOVEMENT** Explorers took different routes across the Atlantic. Who sailed to South America?

the east coast of Mexico with more than 650 soldiers. He was helped by **Malintzin** (mah•LINT•chin), a Native American. She served as his translator.

Cortés captured the Aztec emperor Motecuhzoma. He then destroyed Tenochtitlán. In its place, the Spanish built Mexico City. The city became the capital of Spain's new empire.

In 1531, explorer **Francisco Pizarro** (frahn•SEES•koh pee•SAR•roh) made the first of several unsuccessful attempts to reach Cuzco. He wanted to find Inca gold. Pizarro captured **Atahuallpa** (ah•tah•WAHL•pah), the Inca emperor, in 1532. Atahuallpa refused to accept Christianity or Spanish rule. Pizarro killed him and conquered the Inca Empire.

The Aztec and the Inca could not defend themselves. The Europeans had guns, cannons, and horses, and they did not. Many Aztec and Inca died in battle. They also died of diseases brought by the conquistadors.

READING CHECK ☼SUMMARIZE
How did the line of demarcation affect European exploration of Latin America?

The Northwest Passage

At about the same time, the French and the English were looking for a Northwest Passage they believed existed through Canada. The **Northwest Passage** was supposed to be a water route in North America. It was thought to connect the Atlantic and the Pacific Oceans.

English Explorers

In 1497, the king of England hired an Italian explorer named Giovanni Caboto, or **John Cabot**. The king wanted Cabot to claim land in the Caribbean. Cabot sailed farther to the north. He landed on the coast of what is now Newfoundland.

Back in England, Cabot described a place with an amazing number of fish. He was probably describing the waters of the Grand Banks, located southeast of Newfoundland.

In 1610, an English trading company hired **Henry Hudson** to search for the Northwest Passage. Hudson sailed into a waterway that became known as Hudson Bay. Although Hudson did not find the Northwest Passage, the English claimed the area around Hudson Bay.

During the winter, Hudson's ship became caught in the ice. The angry crew set Hudson, his son, and seven others adrift in a small boat. Then they sailed back to England without them.

▶ **NORTHWEST PASSAGE** English explorer Martin Frobisher met the Inuit at Baffin Island while searching for the Northwest Passage in 1576.

French Explorers

In 1524, the French sent Giovanni Verrazano (vair•uh•ZAH•noh) to look for the Northwest Passage. Verrazano sailed from what is now New York to present-day Nova Scotia but did not find the passage.

Ten years later, the French king sent **Jacques Cartier** (ZHAHK kar•TYAY) to search for the passage. On his first trip, Cartier landed on a peninsula near the mouth of the St. Lawrence River and met the Micmac people.

On his second trip, Cartier traveled inland on the St. Lawrence River. There, he met the Huron people. On his third trip, he once again sailed inland on the St. Lawrence River. This time, he set up camp near **Quebec** city.

READING CHECK **SUMMARIZE**

What did French and British explorers want to find in Canada?

REVIEW

1. **WHAT TO KNOW** Why did Europeans explore Canada and Latin America, and what did they find?

2. **VOCABULARY** Use **conquistador** in a sentence about Spanish exploration.

3. **HISTORY** For what was Columbus searching when he sailed the Atlantic?

4. **CULTURE** What were some of the effects of Pizarro's conquest of the Inca Empire?

5. **CRITICAL THINKING** Why do you think that explorers kept looking for the Northwest Passage?

6. **WRITE A JOURNAL ENTRY** Imagine you are an explorer looking for the Northwest Passage. Write a journal entry describing your first contact with the Inuit people.

Time

1450

1750

1608
The French start
a colony at Quebec

1670
The English start a
colony in Rupert's Land

WHAT TO KNOW

Why did France and England start colonies in Canada?

VOCABULARY

colony p. 35
alliance p. 35
coureur de bois p. 36
voyageur p. 36
Métis p. 36
seigneur p. 37
missionary p. 37
Acadian p. 39

PEOPLE

Samuel de Champlain
Jean Talon
Jacques Marquette
Louis Joliet
Sieur de La Salle

PLACES

Quebec
Montreal
New France
Louisiana
Rupert's Land
Halifax

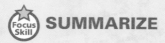

SUMMARIZE

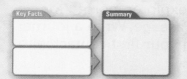

Colonial Life in Canada

YOU ARE THERE

The year is 1614 in the settlement of **Quebec**. You are tired from sawing wood all afternoon. For the past week, you have been helping build a new wall around the settlement.

Next week, you hope to join the group that is building a new warehouse. You have also heard of plans to start clearing land to build a small chapel and a bakery.

Trading furs

Carrying supplies

The Colony of New France

In 1608, the French explorer **Samuel de Champlain** (sham•PLAYN) founded the settlement of Quebec. The settlement was located along the St. Lawrence River. Quebec was the first French colony in North America. A **colony** is a settlement ruled by another country. The king of France wanted to start colonies in North America to protect land claims and trade there.

Fur Trade

The king gave a group of wealthy merchants control over Canada's fur trade. The group then hired Champlain to start a colony at what is now Quebec city. In 1612, the group named Champlain governor. As governor, Champlain had the power to make laws, fight wars, and enter into trade agreements.

Champlain made an **alliance**, or formal partnership, with the Huron and Algonkin. The Native Canadians brought beaver and other animal skins to Quebec to trade for blankets, beads, and other goods. The French sold the furs to make into hats and coats in Europe. Beavers were scarce there, so the furs brought a high price.

> **SAMUEL DE CHAMPLAIN**

Settlement of Quebec

ILLUSTRATION The building was used to store trade goods. What materials were used to make the building?

Building a wall

Splitting and sawing wood

▶ **THE INTENDANT** lived in this palace built in Quebec in 1727. The lawn was used for army training, parades, and other public events.

Voyageurs

In time, some French trappers began to live in Native Canadian villages. These trappers were called **coureurs de bois** (koo•RER duh BWAH), which means "runners of the woods" in French. The coureurs de bois adopted Native Canadian customs and languages.

French traders called **voyageurs** (voy•ah•ZHERZ) carried beaver pelts along the St. Lawrence River in birchbark canoes. Many voyageurs had children with Native Canadian women. Their children were called **Métis** (MAY•tee). The Métis developed their own language, clothing, and art.

New France

In 1642, the French started the settlement of **Montreal** farther inland on the St. Lawrence River, west of Quebec. As more new settlements were built, the king of France made the region one large colony. In 1663, the colony was named **New France**.

A governor and a lawmaking council ruled the colony. The governor and the local Roman Catholic bishop chose the council members. The king sent an intendant to supervise the leaders.

In 1665, **Jean Talon** (zhahn ta•LOHN) became the first intendant. He got the name "the Great Intendant" for creating new jobs and attracting more people to New France. Talon started a shipbuilding yard in Quebec. He also set up Canada's whaling and mining industries.

Seigneurs and Habitants

France wanted settlers to farm along the St. Lawrence River. One of the king's advisers came up with a plan to give large pieces of land to wealthy people called seigneurs. A **seigneur** (sen•YER) rented land to farmers called habitants (a•bee•tahnz). The habitants had to send their grain to a mill owned by the seigneur.

Missionaries

In the early 1600s, the French required that all colonists sent to New France belong to the Roman Catholic Church. Many Protestants who did not want to become Catholics went to English settlements along the Atlantic coast.

Roman Catholic priests called **missionaries** were sent to teach Christianity to Native Canadians. In 1673, **Jacques Marquette** (mar•KET), a missionary from Quebec, sailed south on the Mississippi River with **Louis Joliet** (zhohl•YAY). They were searching

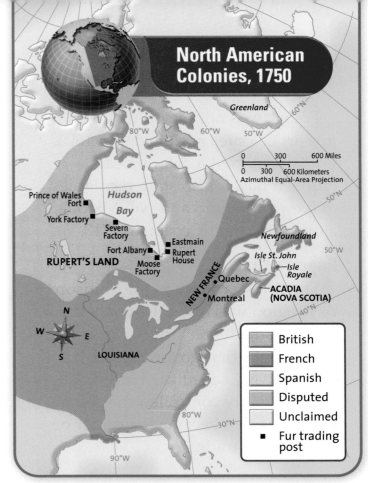

North American Colonies, 1750

British
French
Spanish
Disputed
Unclaimed
■ Fur trading post

MAP SKILL **REGIONS** By 1750, European kingdoms had claimed much of North America. What two kingdoms claimed land in Canada?

for the Northwest Passage. Instead, they reached what is today the state of Mississippi.

In 1682, René-Robert Cavelier (ruh•NAY roh•BAIR ka•vuhl•YAY), **Sieur de La Salle**, traveled all the way to the mouth of the Mississippi. La Salle claimed for France the land whose rivers drained into the Mississippi. This land was called **Louisiana**.

READING CHECK ☼SUMMARIZE

What was the main kind of trade in the colony of New France?

> SIEUR DE LA SALLE

British Colonies

France was not the only kingdom to start colonies in Canada. In 1670, England started a colony near Hudson Bay. It also started colonies in Newfoundland and Nova Scotia, along the Atlantic coast, in 1713.

Rupert's Land

The British colony in the Hudson Bay region was called **Rupert's Land**. It was named after Prince Rupert, the colony's first governor. The trading company called the Hudson's Bay Company controlled the colony. Rupert's Land became the center of Britain's fur trade.

Nova Scotia

In 1713, France was defeated in wars in North America and in Europe. As part of the peace settlement, the British took control of Nova Scotia and Newfoundland. The French remained in control of Île St. Jean (EEL san ZHAHN) and Île Royale (EEL rwah•YAL). These two islands are now known as Prince Edward Island and Cape Breton Island.

In 1719, the French began to build Fort Louisbourg (LOO•ee•boorg) on Île Royale. The British built a fort in the fishing village of **Halifax**, to the south. In 1749, Halifax became the capital of Nova Scotia.

▶ **PRINCE OF WALES FORT** The Hudson's Bay Company built this large stone fort in what is now Churchill, Manitoba, in 1731.

▶ **FISH caught along the coast of Nova Scotia were dried and preserved to be sold in Europe.**

In 1758, British settlers voted for representatives to the Halifax assembly. It was Canada's first elected government.

The Acadians

The French had fought a series of battles against the British for control of the region. As a result, Nova Scotia changed hands several times. By the early 1700s, many French-speaking settlers called **Acadians** (uh•KAY•dee•uhnz) lived in Nova Scotia.

READING CHECK ⓈSUMMARIZE
Where in Canada did the British set up colonies?

REVIEW

1. WHAT TO KNOW Why did France and England start colonies in Canada?

2. VOCABULARY Write a sentence describing the relationship between a **seigneur** and an habitant.

3. CIVICS AND GOVERNMENT What kingdoms ruled Nova Scotia in the 1700s?

4. HISTORY How did alliances with Native Canadians help New France?

5. CRITICAL THINKING Why did Europeans start colonies along the St. Lawrence River?

6. ✎ **WRITE A NEWSPAPER STORY** Imagine that you are a reporter visiting New France. Write an article describing the area and the people's daily work and activities.

Time
1450 — 1750

1535
Spain creates
Viceroyalty
of New Spain

1543
Spain creates
Viceroyalty
of Peru

WHAT TO KNOW
What was life like for
different groups in colonial
Latin America?

VOCABULARY
viceroyalty p. 41
peninsular p. 42
creole p. 42
mestizo p. 42
mulatto p. 42
slavery p. 43
triangular trade p. 43
hacienda p. 43
self-sufficient p. 43
missions p. 44
El Camino Real p. 44
presidio p. 44

PEOPLE
Bartolomé de Las Casas
Juana Inés de la Cruz

PLACES
Viceroyalty of New Spain
Viceroyalty of Peru
Viceroyalty of Brazil

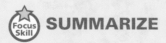

Colonial Life in Latin America

YOU ARE THERE
The year is 1700. You are strolling through the main square in Mexico City. Suddenly, you hear the clatter of hoofs. You jump aside as a horse-drawn carriage turns the corner.

A group of people dressed in expensive clothing is following the carriage. The people look important. They seem to be heading for the palace. Could the rider in the carriage be a new leader?

Viceroyalties

Spain and Portugal built three large colonies, called viceroyalties, in Latin America. A **viceroyalty** is a colony ruled by a representative of the king called a viceroy, or governor.

After the Spanish conquered the Aztec and Inca Empires, they divided the region into the **Viceroyalty of New Spain** and the **Viceroyalty of Peru**. The Viceroyalty of New Spain covered what is today Mexico and parts of Central America and the Caribbean islands. The Viceroyalty of Peru covered the western part of South America.

In 1654, Portugal gained control of Dutch land in what is now northern Brazil. Portugal's colony in the northeastern part of South America became the **Viceroyalty of Brazil.**

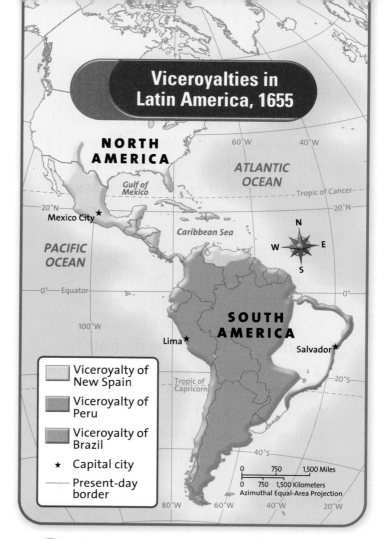

Viceroyalties in Latin America, 1655

NORTH AMERICA

ATLANTIC OCEAN

Gulf of Mexico

Tropic of Cancer

Mexico City ★

Caribbean Sea

PACIFIC OCEAN

Equator

SOUTH AMERICA

Lima ★

Salvador ★

Tropic of Capricorn

Viceroyalty of New Spain

Viceroyalty of Peru

Viceroyalty of Brazil

★ Capital city

Present-day border

0   750   1,500 Miles
0   750   1,500 Kilometers
Azimuthal Equal-Area Projection

MAP SKILL **REGIONS** Mexico City (below) was the capital of New Spain. What were the capitals of the other viceroyalties?

Social Classes

The people who lived in Latin America's colonies belonged to different social classes. A social class is a group of people who are alike in some way. Members of each social class were treated with a different level of respect.

In Spanish colonies, the top social class was made up of peninsulares. A **peninsular** (pay•neen•soo•LAHR) is someone born in Spain. Viceroys, plantation owners, mine operators, and some Catholic priests were peninsulares.

Most of the local leaders who helped the viceroys run Spain's colonial government were wealthy creoles.

A **creole** (KREE•ohl) was a person born to Spanish parents in Mexico. Although some creoles gained more wealth than peninsulares, they could not become viceroys.

The peninsulares and creoles made up only one-tenth of Spain's total colonial population. Yet they had control over the Native Americans, mestizos, mulattoes, and African people. A **mestizo** (meh•STEE•zoh) is someone of mixed Spanish and Native American background. A **mulatto** (myoo•LAH•toh) is someone of both African and European backgrounds.

READING CHECK   **SUMMARIZE**
What were the main social classes in colonial Latin America?

▶ **WEALTHY MESTIZOS** wore clothing and shoes made of velvet and silk.

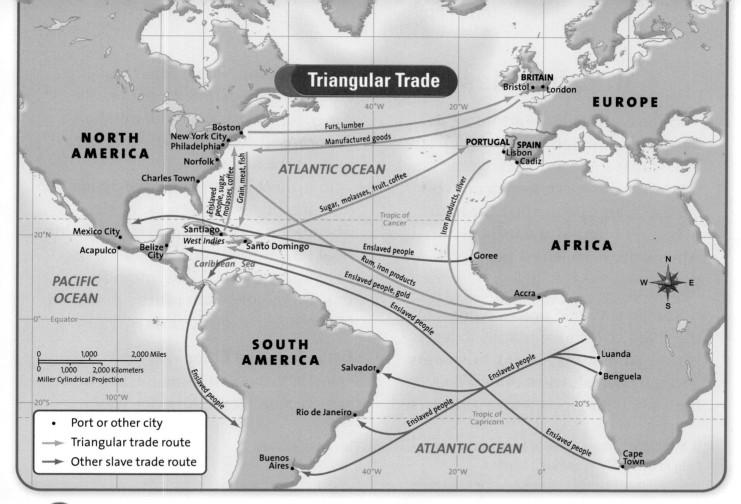

Triangular Trade

Map labels:
BRITAIN — Bristol • London
EUROPE
PORTUGAL • SPAIN — Lisbon • Cadiz
NORTH AMERICA — Boston, New York City, Philadelphia, Norfolk, Charles Town
Mexico City, Acapulco, Belize City, Santiago, West Indies, Santo Domingo
PACIFIC OCEAN
ATLANTIC OCEAN
AFRICA — Goree, Accra, Luanda, Benguela, Cape Town
Caribbean Sea
SOUTH AMERICA — Salvador, Rio de Janeiro, Buenos Aires
Equator
Tropic of Cancer
Tropic of Capricorn

Trade route labels: Furs, lumber; Manufactured goods; Enslaved people, sugar, molasses, coffee; Grain, meat, fish; Sugar, molasses, fruit, coffee; Iron products, silver; Enslaved people; Rum, iron products; Enslaved people, gold; Enslaved people

Legend:
• Port or other city
→ Triangular trade route
→ Other slave trade route

0   1,000   2,000 Miles
0   1,000   2,000 Kilometers
Miller Cylindrical Projection

MAP SKILL — **MOVEMENT** The Americas were connected to Europe and Africa by trade routes. From what places in Africa did enslaved people sail to the Americas?

Slavery in the Americas

Spanish and Portuguese colonists forced Native Americans into slavery. **Slavery** is the practice of holding people against their will and making them work without pay. As the colonies grew, more workers were needed. In the early 1500s, the first enslaved Africans arrived in Brazil.

Triangular Trade

The sale of enslaved Africans was part of the **triangular trade**. First, Europeans went to Africa and traded manufactured goods for slaves. They then sailed to the Americas and traded the enslaved Africans for goods such as sugar and coffee. Those goods were then taken back to Europe, completing the triangle.

Haciendas

Some enslaved people worked on large estates called **haciendas** (ah•see•EN•dahs). Large haciendas were **self-sufficient**, or self-supporting, communities. They had their own churches, gardens, and workshops. Ranchers on the haciendas raised their own livestock and grew their own crops.

READING CHECK ☼SUMMARIZE
How did Latin American slavery change over time?

Missionaries

In the early 1500s, **Bartolomé de Las Casas** (bar•toh•loh•MAY day lahs KAH•sahs) spoke out against the cruel treatment of Native American workers. Las Casas persuaded the king of Spain to outlaw the use of Native Americans as enslaved people.

Missions

Roman Catholic priests were sent to the colonies as missionaries to teach Native Americans about Christianity and the Spanish ways of life. They built small religious settlements, called **missions** near Native American villages. The Spanish forced Native Americans to work on the missions. This caused some Native Americans to fight the Spanish.

To protect its missions, the Spanish built a road system across Mexico. The road system was called **El Camino Real** (el kah•MEE•noh ray•AHL), or "The Royal Road." El Camino Real linked missions with nearby **presidios** (pray•SEE•dee•ohs), or forts.

Cathedrals and Cities

In 1573, the first Roman Catholic cathedral in North America was

▶ **MISSIONS** Many cities in Mexico began as missions. This mission was built in the 1700s in northern Mexico.

completed in Mexico City. The large church was built at the north end of the city's central plaza. The plaza was a large outdoor area where people could gather. The viceroy's palace stood at the other end of the plaza.

The Roman Catholic Church ran the schools of Mexico City. In 1551, the Church helped set up the first university in North America. Today, the university is called the National Autonomous University of Mexico. It is the largest public university in Mexico.

Juana Inés de la Cruz

In 1658, **Juana Inés de la Cruz** (WAHN•ah ee•NES day lah CROOZ) wanted to enter the University of Mexico. Only men could study there. Women were expected to stay at home and take care of their families.

Juana Inés de la Cruz decided to become a nun. She taught herself to read and write and published many poems and essays.

READING CHECK **MAIN IDEA AND DETAILS**
Why were missionaries sent to Latin American colonies?

▶ **JUANA INÉS DE LA CRUZ** supported women's rights in some of her writings.

REVIEW

1. WHAT TO KNOW What was life like for different groups in colonial Latin America?

2. VOCABULARY Use the words **peninsular** and **creole** in a sentence about Spanish viceroys.

3. CULTURE What contributions did missionaries make to life in Latin America?

4. HISTORY How did the El Camino Real help protect missions?

5. CRITICAL THINKING How do you think the triangular trade affected Latin America's sugar trade?

6. 🖌️ **DRAW A HACIENDA** Draw a hacienda, using information in this lesson.

Review and Test Prep

Vocabulary

Identify the term from the word bank that correctly matches each definition.

1. any of the Spanish conquerors in the Americas during the early 1500s

2. a road system that was built through Mexico between missions and forts

3. a French trader

4. planning and following a route

5. a settlement ruled by another country

6. a French-speaking person who lived in British-controlled Nova Scotia

7. Canadians of French and Native Canadian backgrounds

8. a large estate in a Spanish colony

Word Bank

navigation p. 29	**Métis** p. 36
conquistador p. 30	**Acadian** p. 39
colony p. 35	**hacienda** p. 43
voyageur p. 36	**El Camino Real** p. 44

Facts and Main Ideas

Answer these questions.

9. Which native emperor was captured and killed by Pizarro?

10. Where did Protestants in colonial Canada go if they did not want to become Catholics?

11. What were the goals of the Spanish conquistadors?

12. Where was the first Roman Catholic cathedral in North America built?

Write the letter of the best choice.

13. Near which of these places did John Cabot see large numbers of fish?
   A Newfoundland
   B Quebec
   C Brazil
   D Florida

14. Which of these explorers sailed to the mouth of the Mississippi?
   A Jean Talon
   B Sieur de La Salle
   C Louis Joliet
   D Samuel de Champlain

15. What did Bartolomé de las Casas speak out against?
   A the building of presidios
   B the triangular trade
   C teaching the native peoples Christianity
   D the cruel treatment of Native American workers

Critical Thinking

16. What role did missionaries play in colonial Canada and Latin America?

17. Why do you think the French king allowed merchants to start the Quebec colony?

writing

Write a Narrative Imagine that you are a European explorer arriving in the land now known as Canada. Write a narrative story describing the challenges you faced on your voyage to the Americas.

Revolution and Independence

CHAPTER 3

INDEPENDENCE MONUMENT,
MEXICO CITY, MEXICO

LESSON 1
Colonial Unrest

LESSON 2
Independence

LESSON 3
Building Nations

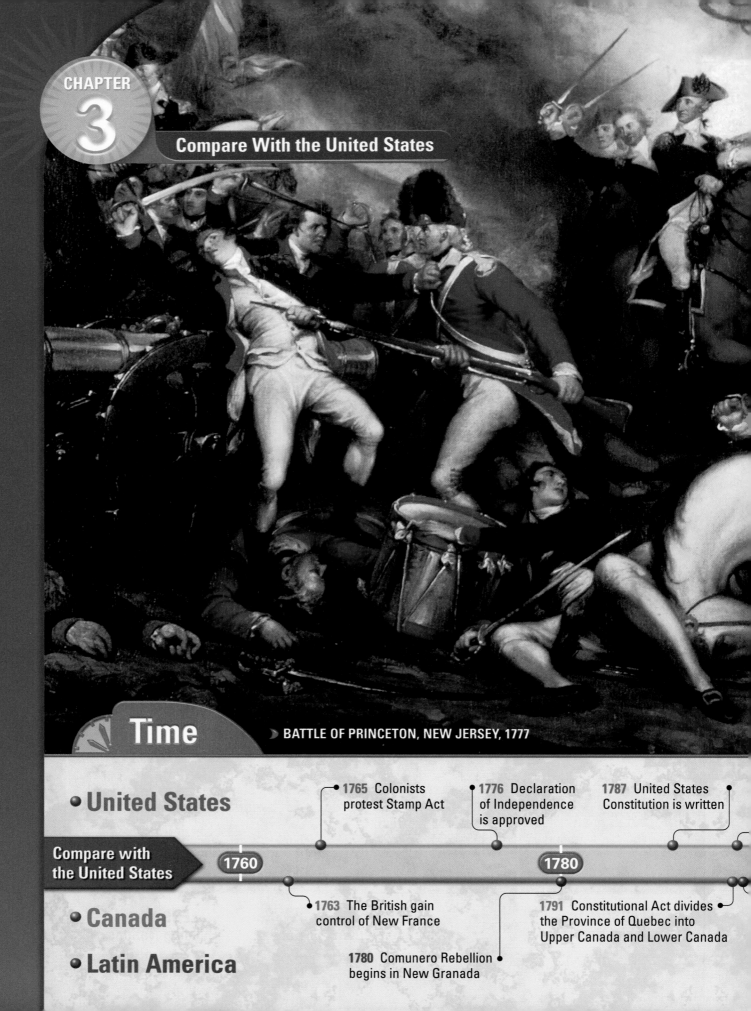

Time

▶ BATTLE OF PRINCETON, NEW JERSEY, 1777

● **United States**

1765 Colonists protest Stamp Act

1776 Declaration of Independence is approved

1787 United States Constitution is written

Compare with the United States

1760

1780

● **Canada**

1763 The British gain control of New France

1791 Constitutional Act divides the Province of Quebec into Upper Canada and Lower Canada

● **Latin America**

1780 Comunero Rebellion begins in New Granada

1791 Bill of Rights added to the Constitution

1803 Louisiana purchased from France

1812 War of 1812 begins

1800

1820

1840

1837 Louis-Joseph Papineau and William Lyon Mackenzie lead rebellions

1840 Act of Union unites Upper Canada and Lower Canada

1791 Toussaint-Louverture leads revolt in French colony of St. Domingue

1810 Miguel Hidalgo calls for Mexico's independence from Spain

1819 Simón Bolívar leads revolution in New Granada

1821 Mexico wins independence

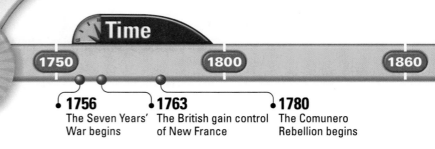

Time

1750   1800   1860

1756   **1763**   **1780**
The Seven Years'   The British gain control   The Comunero
War begins   of New France   Rebellion begins

💡 **WHAT TO KNOW**
What caused conflicts in the colonies of Canada and Latin America?

VOCABULARY
confederation p. 51
Quebec Act p. 53
Comunero Rebellion p. 55

PEOPLE
Samuel de Champlain
James Wolfe
Louis-Joseph de Montcalm
Tupac Amarú II

PLACES
Ohio River valley
Plains of Abraham
Louisiana
New Granada
Río de la Plata
Bogotá

 **CAUSE AND EFFECT**

Colonial Unrest

YOU ARE THERE
Your canoe glides through the clear waters of the St. Lawrence River. Bundled in the boat's center is a heavy load of beaver furs. You and your companion are taking a chance sneaking through Iroquois territory. You scan the thick forests along the riverbanks, shivering at the thought of a hidden enemy. You look forward to arriving at the trading post. There, you will exchange the furs for fresh vegetables and cooking pots.

Conflict Over Fur Trade

In 1609, **Samuel de Champlain** led Huron warriors in the first of many battles against the Iroquois. The Huron served as agents for the French in the fur trade.

The Huron people lived north of the St. Lawrence River. The Iroquois lived to the south, in what is now New York state.

The Huron spoke the same language as the Iroquois and followed many of the same customs. Yet the two were bitter enemies.

The Iroquois War

To help protect themselves, the Huron formed a confederation. A **confederation** is a loose group of governments acting together. The Huron confederation was made up of Huron, Algonkin, and Montagnais tribes.

After years of trapping, the Iroquois had exhausted the supply of beaver from their own lands. They wanted to take control of the Huron's fur trade.

By the 1630s, the Iroquois had bought European weapons from Dutch traders. This gave them an advantage in their wars with the Huron. The Iroquois drove the Huron away from their villages along the St. Lawrence River in the 1640s.

At about this time, the English formed an alliance with the Iroquois. In doing this, the English hoped to gain control of French land and trading routes.

READING CHECK ⟳ **CAUSE AND EFFECT**
Why did the Iroquois attack the Huron?

❯ **ILLUSTRATION A Huron guide helps voyageurs escape Iroquois attacks.**

▶ **BATTLE OF QUEBEC** In 1759, General James Wolfe died while leading the British army to victory over the French. This canteen was carried by British soldiers.

The Seven Years' War

By the middle of the 1700s, France and Britain were in a struggle to gain control of North America. In 1754, war broke out over control of the **Ohio River valley.** This land lay west of the Appalachian Mountains.

In the United States, the war is called the French and Indian War. In Canada, it is called the Seven Years' War because it lasted from 1756 to 1763 there.

At first, the French won their battles against the British. The French had learned fighting styles from their Native Canadian allies. They attacked from the cover of the forests. The British could not protect themselves from their hidden attackers. They were used to fighting in open fields. Still,

the French could not defeat Britain's much larger army.

The Battle of Quebec in 1759 was a turning point in the war. British General **James Wolfe** and 9,000 soldiers attacked Quebec. They surprised the French army of General **Louis-Joseph de Montcalm** by climbing the steep cliffs west of Quebec. In less than half an hour, the British soldiers defeated the French on the **Plains of Abraham,** on top of the cliffs.

The British captured Montreal in 1760. In 1763, the French agreed to hand over to the British their land in Canada.

The Acadians

At about this time, the Acadians were still living in British-controlled Nova Scotia. The Acadians did not fight in the Seven Years' War. Even so, the British did not trust them. They forced the Acadians from their homes.

Many Acadians went to France or to Britain. Thousands of others settled in **Louisiana**, which was under Spanish control.

The Quebec Act

After the Seven Years' War, the British allowed many French colonists to stay in Canada. The British changed the name of the colony of New France to the Province of Quebec.

In 1774, the British passed a law called the **Quebec Act**. The law gave the French people who stayed in the British colony the right to keep their own language, their Roman Catholic religion, and many of their laws.

READING CHECK ⦿ **CAUSE AND EFFECT**
Why did the French and the British fight the Seven Years' War?

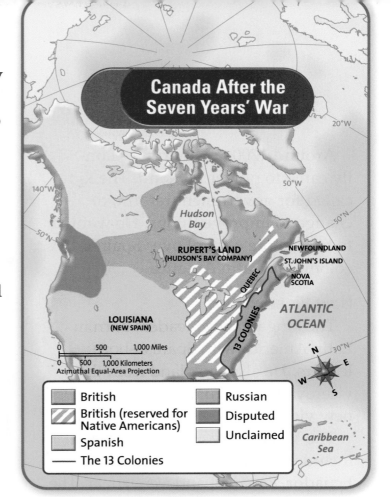

Canada After the Seven Years' War

Legend	
British	Russian
British (reserved for Native Americans)	Disputed
Spanish	Unclaimed
— The 13 Colonies	

MAP SKILL **REGIONS** The British controlled Canada after the Seven Years' War. Which country claimed Louisiana?

FAST FACT

The Acadians are the ancestors of the Cajuns (KAY•juhnz), who now live in southern Louisiana. This painting shows the British ordering the Acadians to leave their homes in 1755.

Changes in New Spain

Around 1700, a new ruling family came to power in Spain. The king called for government reform, or change to improve things. He wanted to have more control over Spain's colonies in Latin America.

New Viceroyalties

The king replaced leaders born in Latin America with Spanish-born leaders. He also took land from the viceroyalty of Peru to create two new viceroyalties.

The Viceroyalty of **New Granada** included what is today Colombia, Ecuador, Panama, and Venezuela. The Viceroyalty of **Río de la Plata** included what is now Argentina, Uruguay, Paraguay, and Bolivia.

New Taxes

The king's reforms called for an increase in the size of New Spain's army. To pay for the the larger army, the new leaders raised taxes in colonial Latin America. Taxes became so high that merchants were forced to charge more for food and other goods.

Spanish Viceroyalties, 1776

NORTH AMERICA

ATLANTIC OCEAN

Gulf of Mexico

Caribbean Sea

PACIFIC OCEAN

SOUTH AMERICA

Viceroyalty of New Granada
Viceroyalty of Río de la Plata
Viceroyalty of Peru
Viceroyalty of New Spain
Present-day border

0   750   1,500 Miles
0   750   1,500 Kilometers
Azimuthal Equal-Area Projection

MAP SKILL **REGIONS** In the 1700s, Spain created two new viceroyalties in Latin America. What viceroyalties were in North America in 1776?

People in the Latin American colonies paid more than twice as much in taxes as people living in Spain.

Tupac Amarú II

In 1780, a wealthy mestizo landowner in Peru named José Gabriel Condorcanqui (kawn•dawr•KAHNG•kee) protested the living conditions of workers. He changed his name to **Tupac Amarú II**. His ancestor was the last Inca emperor.

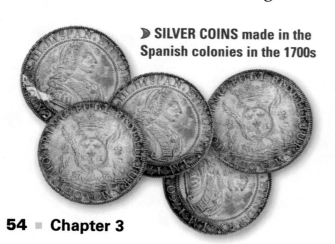

▶ SILVER COINS made in the Spanish colonies in the 1700s

Tupac Amarú II then led an armed revolt. Joining him were Native Americans, mestizos, and creoles. The Spanish army defeated the rebels and put Tupac Amarú II to death.

The Comunero Rebellion

In the same year, a group of farmers in New Granada took action. They marched on **Bogotá**, the capital of New Granada, in what is now Colombia. They wanted lower taxes and better working conditions in the mines. Their protest is called the **Comunero Rebellion**, or Commoners' Rebellion.

At first, the viceroy of New Granada was frightened by the rebels. He agreed to their demands. Later, however, he ordered the leaders arrested. Some were put to death. The viceroy's cruel response to the Comunero Rebellion alarmed people. Many began to think about breaking free from Spanish rule.

READING CHECK Ŏ CAUSE AND EFFECT
What effect did the increase in taxes have on Spanish colonies?

▶ **TUPAC AMARÚ II** is shown here wearing Inca clothing.

REVIEW

1. **WHAT TO KNOW** What caused conflicts in the colonies of Canada and Latin America?

2. **VOCABULARY** What purposes did **confederations** serve in North America?

3. **GEOGRAPHY** What area did the French and British fight over during the Seven Years' War?

4. **CULTURE** What French-speaking people were forced to leave Nova Scotia after the Seven Years' War?

5. **CRITICAL THINKING** Why do you think the battle on the Plains of Abraham was important?

6. ✎ **WRITE A REPORT** Find out more about the Seven Years' War. Choose a topic that interests you related to the war. Then write a one-page report. Share your report with your classmates.

1791
The Constitutional Act divides the Province of Quebec into Upper Canada and Lower Canada

1804
St. Domingue becomes the nation of Haiti

1810
Hidalgo calls for Mexican independence

💡 **WHAT TO KNOW**
How did colonies in Canada and Latin America move toward independence?

VOCABULARY
United Empire Loyalist p. 57
Constitutional Act p. 58
Red River Settlement p. 59
Plan of Iguala p. 61
republic p. 61

PEOPLE
Miguel Hidalgo
Joseph Brandt
Alexander Mackenzie
Toussaint-Louverture
Simón Bolívar
Agustín de Iturbide
Guadalupe Victoria

PLACES
Quebec
New Brunswick
Alberta
Manitoba

CAUSE AND EFFECT

Independence

YOU ARE THERE It is the morning of September 16, 1810. You are in the village of Dolores in New Spain. The church bells are ringing in the town. A crowd has gathered outside the church. The village priest, **Miguel Hidalgo** (ee•DAHL•goh), is talking to the crowd about equal rights for all and an end to Spanish rule. Your heart races. People shout, "Long live Mexico! Death to bad government!"

▶ **MIGUEL HIDALGO** calls for independence at Dolores in 1810.

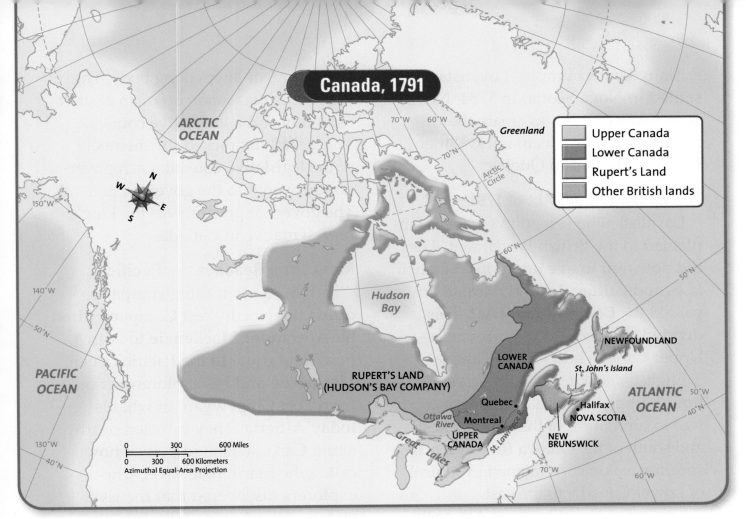

Canada, 1791

Legend:
- Upper Canada
- Lower Canada
- Rupert's Land
- Other British lands

ARCTIC OCEAN

Greenland

Hudson Bay

RUPERT'S LAND (HUDSON'S BAY COMPANY)

PACIFIC OCEAN

ATLANTIC OCEAN

NEWFOUNDLAND

LOWER CANADA

St. John's Island

Quebec

Montreal

Ottawa River

UPPER CANADA

Great Lakes

St. Lawrence R.

NEW BRUNSWICK

Halifax

NOVA SCOTIA

0   300   600 Miles
0   300   600 Kilometers
Azimuthal Equal-Area Projection

MAP SKILL MOVEMENT Many loyalists moved into the area north of the Great Lakes. What province was located just north of the Great Lakes in 1791?

Changes in Canada

The colonists in North America's 13 colonies did not like being taxed without representation. They began fighting against Britain in 1775. In time, the Americans won their war of independence. Canada still remained a loyal British colony. Yet Canada's relationship to Britain slowly began to change.

Americans Invade Canada

At the beginning of the American Revolution, American troops attacked British forces in Canada. General Richard Montgomery marched into Montreal and then joined General Benedict Arnold in an attempt to capture **Quebec**. British forces led by Guy Carleton, the governor of Quebec, held off the Americans. Then more British soldiers arrived. They were able to force the Americans back to New York.

United Empire Loyalists

During the American Revolution, thousands of American colonists loyal to Britain fled north to Canada. These emigrants were known as **United Empire Loyalists**. They were joined by formerly enslaved Africans and Iroquois, led by Chief **Joseph Brandt**.

Many United Empire Loyalists settled in Nova Scotia. In 1784, Nova Scotia was divided to create the province of **New Brunswick**. Other Loyalists moved to Quebec.

The Constitutional Act of 1791

Loyalists who settled in Quebec complained to the British Parliament. They did not want to live under local French laws and culture. In 1791, Parliament passed the **Constitutional Act**. This divided Quebec into two provinces—Upper Canada and Lower Canada.

English-speaking colonists controlled Upper Canada. This province was located north of the Great Lakes and south of the Ottawa River. French-speaking colonists remained in control of Lower Canada, to the east.

Under the Constitutional Act, each province had a governor and a legislature, or lawmaking body. The legislature was made up of an elected assembly and a legislative council. The governors picked the members of the legislative council. Each governor answered to the governor general. The governor general was the king's representative in Canada.

Mackenzie Reaches the Pacific

In 1789, a fur-trading company called the North West Company hired Sir **Alexander Mackenzie** to search for a land route to the Pacific Ocean. Mackenzie and his explorers set out from Fort Chipewyan, in what is today **Alberta**. They traveled north along Canada's longest river, now called the Mackenzie River. The explorers discovered that the river ended at the Arctic Ocean, not the Pacific.

▶ THE EXPLORER Sir Alexander Mackenzie (right) stopped at this spot (below) in British Columbia before he reached the Pacific Ocean in 1793.

▶ **THE BATTLE OF QUEENSTON HEIGHTS** was a major victory for Canada in the War of 1812.

In the fall of 1792, Mackenzie set out on the Peace River. Almost a year later, he reached the Pacific Ocean. His journey opened up the western half of British North America to trade and settlement.

The War of 1812

In the early 1800s, the United States thought that the British were supplying Native Americans in the Ohio River valley with guns. In the War of 1812, the United States fought against Britain. To protect itself, the United States invaded Canada. At the Battle of Queenston Heights, the British and Canadian troops defeated the Americans. Canada's show of strength helped create national pride and unity.

The Red River Settlement

After the war, some settlers moved west into the **Red River Settlement**. This became the first settlement northwest of Lake Superior. Scottish and Irish fur traders claimed land in the northern part. The southern part was settled by the Métis.

To protect their way of life, the Métis blocked the movement of settlers into the Red River valley. In 1870, the Canadian government accepted their claim. The Red River Settlement became part of the province of **Manitoba**.

READING CHECK ☉ **CAUSE AND EFFECT**
How did the Métis react to migration into the Red River valley?

Revolutions in Latin America

The American Revolution helped lead to independence in Latin America. In the early 1800s, Haiti, Venezuela, Mexico, Bolivia, Ecuador, Brazil, and Uruguay all became independent countries.

Haiti

In 1791, a former slave named **Toussaint-Louverture** (too•SAHN loo•vair•TYUR) led a rebellion. He and others stood up against the colonial government of the French colony of St. Domingue. The French calmed the rebels by ending slavery and appointing Toussaint-Louverture governor.

Napoleon Bonaparte became the new leader of France in 1802. He tried to take back St. Domingue and had Toussaint-Louverture arrested. The

▶ TOUSSAINT-LOUVERTURE

people of St. Domingue rebelled. They won independence in 1804. Their new nation changed its name to Haiti. It was the first nation in Latin America to win its freedom.

Venezuela

In 1819, a wealthy landowner named **Simón Bolívar** (see•MOHN boh•LEE•var) led a revolution in New Granada. As a result, New Granada became an independent state called Gran Colombia. Bolívar's army defeated the Spanish in what is now Venezuela in 1821. Venezuela broke away from Gran Colombia in 1829 and became an independent nation in 1830.

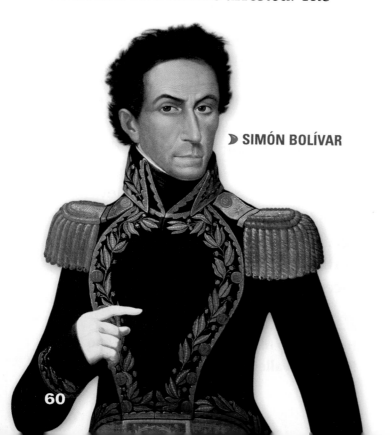

▶ SIMÓN BOLÍVAR

▶ **AGUSTÍN DE ITURBIDE** enters Mexico City in September 1821 after defeating the Spanish army.

Mexican Independence

In New Spain, Miguel Hidalgo led a rebellion against the Spanish government. Hidalgo's fight for independence brought about other uprisings in the colony.

For the next ten years, rebels fought to take over New Spain. However, the Spanish army was too strong. Then, in 1821, a Spanish army leader named **Agustín de Iturbide** (ee•ter•BEE•day) changed sides. Iturbide and the rebels easily defeated the Spanish army.

Iturbide announced a new plan of government called the **Plan of Iguala** (ee•GWAH•lah). Under this plan, New Spain became the independent empire of Mexico. The plan also gave equal rights to everyone.

In 1824, Mexico adopted a new constitution that made it a republic. A **republic** is a form of government in which people elect representatives to govern the country. **Guadalupe Victoria**, a former soldier, was elected Mexico's first president.

READING CHECK 〇**CAUSE AND EFFECT**
How did events in the United States affect colonial Latin America?

REVIEW

1. **WHAT TO KNOW** How did colonies in Canada and Latin America move toward independence?

2. **VOCABULARY** Describe the role that **United Empire Loyalists** had in the creation of the **Constitutional Act**.

3. **HISTORY** Which Latin American nation gained its independence first?

4. **CULTURE** How did the War of 1812 affect Canada?

5. **CRITICAL THINKING** Why do you think Latin Americans became so interested in independence after the American Revolution?

6. ✎ **WRITE A PERSUASIVE LETTER** Write a letter to members of the British Parliament telling them why they should pass the Constitutonal Act.

1837
The British army stops
the Papineau Rebellion

1846
The Mexican-American
War begins

1870
War of the Triple
Alliance ends

WHAT TO KNOW
How did nations in
Canada and Latin America
create new governments?

VOCABULARY
Act of Union p. 64
British North America Act
    p. 64
dominion p. 64
prime minister p. 64
dictator p. 65
Gadsden Purchase p. 66

PEOPLE
Louis-Joseph Papineau
William Lyon Mackenzie
Lord Durham
Antonio López de
    Santa Anna
Benito Juárez
Carlos Antonio López

PLACES
Toronto
Guatemala City

**CAUSE AND
EFFECT**

Building Nations

**YOU
ARE
THERE**
It is December 14, 1837, in the city of
St. Eustache in Lower Canada. You are
walking down the street when you see a group
of people. Several are on horseback. Others are
on foot, holding rifles and pitchforks. You
remember your parents talking about a rebel
uprising. You race home to tell them what you
have just seen.

Union and Self-Government

During the 1830s, many Canadians were unhappy with their colonial government. Two groups took action. **Louis-Joseph Papineau** (pah•pee•NOH) led the Patriot party in Lower Canada. **William Lyon Mackenzie** led the Reform party in Upper Canada.

Papineau sent a list of grievances, or complaints, to the British Parliament. At the very least, he thought that Canadians should be allowed to elect their governor and legislative council.

Rebellions in Upper and Lower Canada

In 1837, Parliament rejected all of Papineau's grievances. To make things worse, Canada faced hard economic times. These things angered the members of the Patriot and Reform parties.

In Lower Canada, armed members of the Patriot party tried to take over Montreal and other cities. The rebellion was quickly put down by the British army.

In Upper Canada, Mackenzie's followers tried to take over **Toronto** but failed. The British army burned the rebels' homes, and the leaders of the rebellion escaped across the border to the United States.

▶ **PAPINEAU REBELLION** The British army battles rebels in St. Eustache in 1837.

The Act of Union

In 1838, the British government sent **Lord Durham** to Canada to look into the rebellions. After five months, he returned to Britain. Back home, he wrote his final *Report on the Affairs of British North America*.

Durham said that Upper and Lower Canada should be united into one province. He thought Canada should have a responsible government. He meant a government that answered to the Canadian people, not to British rulers.

In 1840, the British Parliament passed the **Act of Union**. The law combined Upper Canada and Lower Canada into the United Province of Canada. Upper Canada was renamed Canada West. Lower Canada was called Canada East. Both regions were given the same number of representatives in the legislature.

The Dominion of Canada

In 1867, the British Parliament passed the **British North America Act**. The act served as Canada's first constitution. It united all of Canada into one nation called the Dominion of Canada. A **dominion** is a self-governing nation that gives the British monarch the final word in the country's affairs. Canada had to get the approval of the British Parliament to make any changes to its constitution.

The British North America Act also created Canada's Parliament. It was made up of an elected House of Commons and an appointed Senate. The leader of the government was called the **prime minister**. The Parliament oversaw Canada's courts, laws, and taxes.

READING CHECK ⟳ **CAUSE AND EFFECT**
What actions brought about the Act of Union?

▶ **MEMBERS OF CANADA'S PARLIAMENT** have met in this building in Ottawa since 1867.

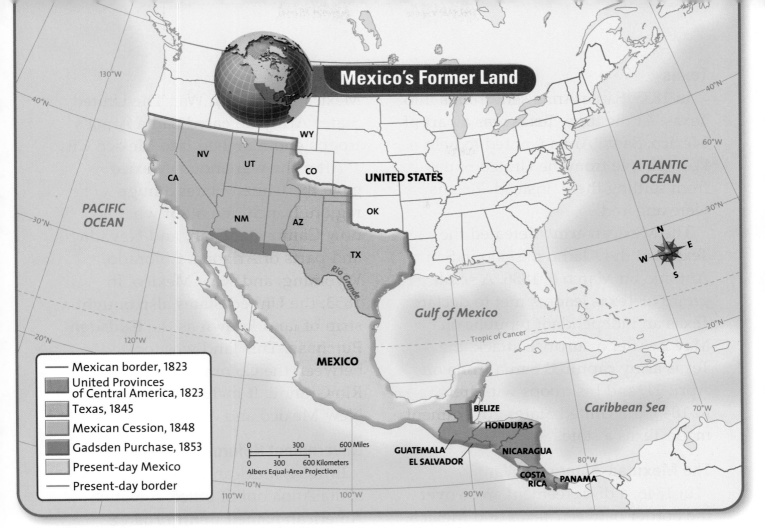

Mexico's Former Land

Legend:
— Mexican border, 1823
■ United Provinces of Central America, 1823
■ Texas, 1845
■ Mexican Cession, 1848
■ Gadsden Purchase, 1853
□ Present-day Mexico
— Present-day border

MAP SKILL **REGIONS** Between 1823 and 1850, Mexico's borders changed many times. Which Central American countries did Mexico once control?

Changes in Latin America

In 1822, Mexico took control of Central America. At that time in history, Mexico's land stretched from Costa Rica in the south to present-day California in the north.

Central America broke away from Mexico in 1823. It then formed a union called the United Provinces of Central America. Leaders from Guatemala, El Salvador, Honduras, Nicaragua, and Costa Rica met in **Guatemala City**, the union's capital city. They approved a constitution that ended slavery. They also elected a president to run the new government. Despite efforts to keep the union together, civil war broke out in 1840. The union broke up, and each province became an independent country.

Santa Anna

In 1833, Mexicans elected General **Antonio López de Santa Anna** as their new president. They wanted him to bring stability to the government. Instead, he made himself dictator. A **dictator** is a ruler who has complete control over government.

Texas

In 1835, Santa Anna sent troops into Texas. At the time, Texas was a part of Mexico. Santa Anna wanted to help keep people from the United States from settling there. Instead, Texans were angered.

The Mexican army defeated the Texans at the Alamo mission in San Antonio on March 6, 1836. A small group of Texas leaders met to declare Texas an independent republic on May 2. After a surprise attack, the Texas army captured Santa Anna on April 21, and his troops withdrew. In 1845, the United States government made Texas a state.

The Mexican-American War

In 1846, a disagreement arose over the border between Texas and Mexico. The United States declared war on Mexico. This war is known as the Mexican-American War. The United States Army defeated Santa Anna's troops and marched into Mexico City.

After the war ended, Mexico gave the United States a huge region. It included all of what is now California, Utah, and Nevada and parts of Arizona, Colorado, Wyoming, and New Mexico. In 1853, the United States also bought a strip of land known as the **Gadsden Purchase**. This land was located between the Colorado River and the Rio Grande. It included the rest of New Mexico and Arizona.

Government Reform

In 1854, Mexican reformers forced Santa Anna out of office. A Native American named **Benito Juárez** helped write a new constitution. Juárez was elected president in 1861.

▶ **BENITO JUÁREZ** helped bring about many changes during his two terms as president.

▶ **WAR OF THE TRIPLE ALLIANCE** This painting shows an Argentine army camp in Paraguay in 1866.

The War of the Triple Alliance

For many years, Paraguay had a strong leader named **Carlos Antonio López** (LOH•pes). López hoped to make his country powerful.

When Carlos López died, Brazil, Argentina, and Uruguay formed an alliance against Paraguay. This alliance was called the Triple Alliance. Over the next five years, the Triple Alliance violently attacked Paraguay.

By 1870, most of the Paraguayan army had been destroyed. The Paraguayan ruler was killed. About 300,000 Paraguayans had died during the war.

READING CHECK ⏰ **CAUSE AND EFFECT**
How did war affect the people of Paraguay?

REVIEW

1. WHAT TO KNOW How did nations in Canada and Latin America create new governments?

2. VOCABULARY Write a sentence describing the **British North America Act**.

3. HISTORY What effect did Lord Durham's report have on Canada's government?

4. CIVICS AND GOVERNMENT How did the British North America Act help make Canada a stronger country?

5. CRITICAL THINKING In what ways do you think Mexico would be different today if Santa Anna had not been elected president?

6. DRAW MAPS Make several maps to show how the size of Canada changed during the 1700s and early 1800s. How did Mexico's experience differ from Canada's during the same time period?

Review and Test Prep

Vocabulary

Identify the term from the word bank that correctly matches each definition.

1. the leader of Canada's government

2. the first Canadian settlement northwest of Lake Superior

3. a law that created the Dominion of Canada

4. a form of government in which people elect representatives

5. a law that combined Upper and Lower Canada

6. governments working together

7. a ruler who has complete control

8. American colonist who supported Britain and fled to Canada

Word Bank

confederation p. 51   **Act of Union** p. 64

United Empire   **British North**
   Loyalist p. 57   **America Act** p. 64

Red River Settlement   **prime minister** p. 64
   p. 59
          dictator p. 65

republic p. 61

Facts and Main Ideas

Answer these questions.

9. What caused the Seven Years' War?

10. Who led a rebellion in Peru in 1780?

11. What revolution set an example for people in South America?

12. Who led an unsuccessful rebellion to take over Toronto?

Write the letter of the best choice.

13. Which of the following lived in Canada?
    A Simón Bolívar
    B the Acadians
    C Toussaint-Louverture
    D the Cajuns

14. Who was the first president of Mexico?
    A General Antonio López de Santa Anna
    B Guadalupe Victoria
    C Miguel Hidalgo
    D Agustín de Iturbide

15. Which country was part of the Triple Alliance?
    A Peru
    B Argentina
    C Colombia
    D Mexico

Critical Thinking

16. Why were alliances with the Iroquois important to the British?

17. Why did the United States declare war on Mexico in the 1840s?

writing

Write a Persuasive Letter Imagine that you are a leader of one of the rebellions against Canada's colonial government in 1837. Write a letter to the people in your homeland giving reasons why they should join the rebellion.

Growth and Change

▶ **CN TOWER, TORONTO ONTARIO, CANADA**

LESSON 1
Expansion and Immigration

LESSON 2
Present-Day Democracies

LESSONS 3 AND 4
Economies of Canada and Latin America

Time

▶ CARGO SHIP IN A PORT IN GEORGIA

1941 The United States enters World War II

1969 United States astronauts land on the moon

2001 Terrorists attack sites in the United States

1950

Present

1982 Canada adopts Charter of Rights and Freedoms

1999 Nunavut becomes a territory

1917 Mexico adopts its present constitution

1948 Organization of American States forms

Time

| 1860 | | | | Present |

1885
The Canadian Pacific
Railway is completed

1896
Gold is discovered
in the Klondike region

1898
The Spanish-American
War is fought

WHAT TO KNOW
How did Canada and
Latin America grow and
change in the late 1800s?

VOCABULARY
gold rush p. 73

Canadian Pacific Railway
p. 73

Mounties p. 74

vaquero p. 75

PLACES
Klondike
British Columbia
Manitoba
Northwest Territories
Montreal
Alberta
Saskatchewan
Yukon
Santiago de Cuba
Havana
São Paulo
Buenos Aires

COMPARE AND CONTRAST

Expansion and Immigration

YOU ARE THERE
You and your uncle are sitting in front
of the fireplace in your home in Ottawa.
"It's sure good to be back," he says, smiling. He
shows you a pickle jar. You see that the jar is full
of sparkling yellow rocks. "It's gold," you whisper.
Your uncle's smile grows bigger. "It's gold!" you
shout. "Tell me how you got it," you beg. "Well, it
all began with a railroad ride across Canada.
I was headed for the **Klondike** region . . . "

▶ **GOLD MINERS** near Dawson City in the
Klondike region in the 1890s

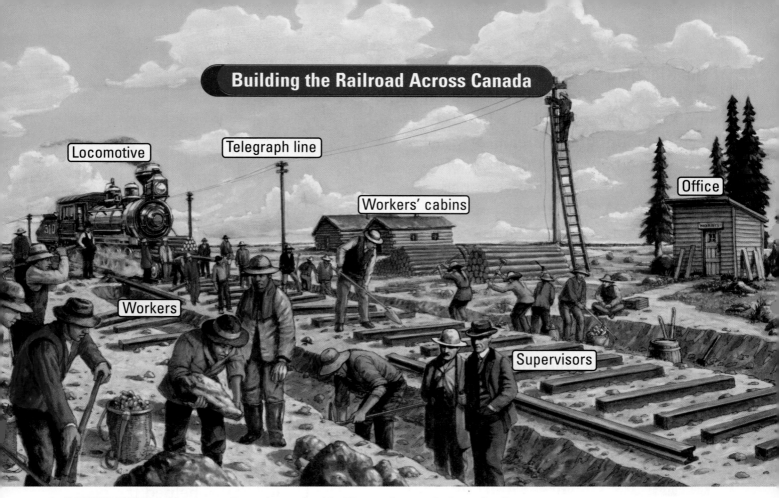

Building the Railroad Across Canada

Locomotive

Telegraph line

Office

Workers' cabins

Workers

Supervisors

▶ **ILLUSTRATION** What inventions shown in this illustration made it easier for people to travel and to communicate across Canada?

Westward Expansion

In 1858, gold was discovered in **British Columbia,** an independent British colony in southwestern Canada. During the **gold rush** of the 1860s, thousands of people searching for gold traveled to the region.

The Canadian government began to worry that the United States might claim British Columbia. Canada needed to persuade British Columbia to become a province. The government did this by promising to build a railroad across Canada.

In the early 1870s, British Columbia became a province. So did **Manitoba.**

Also, land in northern Canada was grouped together as the **Northwest Territories.**

Canadian Pacific Railway

The **Canadian Pacific Railway** was completed in 1885. It stretched from Victoria, British Columbia, to **Montreal,** Quebec. The railroad made it easier for people to travel across the Canadian Shield. It opened up western Canada to new settlement and economic growth.

European immigrants flocked to the Interior Plains. By 1905, enough new people lived there to create the provinces of **Alberta** and **Saskatchewan.**

The Klondike Gold Rush

In 1896, another gold rush started in the Klondike region. The Klondike is a cold, mountainous area near Alaska. At the height of the Klondike gold rush, the new city of Dawson had more than 25,000 settlers.

The Royal Canadian Mounted Police, or **Mounties**, kept the peace in the Klondike during the gold rush. The Mounties were started in the mid-1860s. Today, they serve as Canada's national police force.

The Klondike gold rush lasted only two years. Yet, many people stayed in the area. In 1898, the Canadian government made the Klondike into a new territory called the **Yukon**.

READING CHECK ☼COMPARE AND CONTRAST
What happened to British Columbia and the Yukon after the gold rushes of the 1860s and 1890s?

▶ **THE SPANISH ARMY** surrendered to the United States Army in Santiago de Cuba, in Cuba, on June 17, 1898.

Cuban Independence

The United States helped the people of Cuba win independence from Spain. In 1898, the United States battleship *Maine* exploded in the harbor of **Havana,** Cuba. The cause was never discovered. However, Americans blamed the Spanish for the explosion.

In April, the United States declared war against Spain. American troops marched on the city of **Santiago de Cuba,** in Cuba, and defeated the Spanish. The Spanish-American War ended Spain's claims in the Americas.

READING CHECK ☼COMPARE AND CONTRAST
What reasons did Cuba and the United States have for fighting the Spanish-American War?

▶ **THE MOUNTIES** wear red uniforms in parades and for other special events.

Growth and Change in Mexico

In the late 1800s, thousands of immigrants and farmers moved to Mexico's cities to work in factories. Many of Mexico's factories used steam-powered machines.

Changes in technology and transportation helped the economy grow rapidly. New railroad lines were built connecting rural areas to cities. Raw materials such as cotton were shipped by railroad to factories in the cities. The raw materials were used to make textiles and other manufactured products. Those products were then exported to other countries.

Vaqueros

As the cities grew, the demand for beef increased. In the fall, cowhands called **vaqueros** (vah•KAIR•ohz) rounded up cattle. Then they watched over the cattle during the winter. In the spring, the vaqueros herded the cattle across hundreds of miles to the nearest railroad town. From there, the cattle were shipped east.

Many vaqueros crossed over the border to the United States. They showed cowhands there how to tame wild horses. The cowhands in the United States adopted the vaqueros' language, customs, and clothing.

READING CHECK **MAIN IDEA AND DETAILS**
Why did people move to Mexico's cities in the late 1800s?

▶ **VAQUEROS used lightweight ropes called lassos to round up cattle.**

Immigration to Latin America

In the late 1800s, Europeans and Asians began pouring into Central America, the Caribbean islands, and South America. Most of them were poor. They came to Latin America for a better way of life. Many settled in cities. They brought with them new customs, changing the culture of the places to which they moved.

European Immigration

Italians settled in Argentina, Brazil, and Uruguay. British and Dutch immigrants settled in Belize, Guyana, Suriname, and Jamaica. Between 1880 and 1914, thousands of Jewish people left Russia to escape unfair treatment. More than 100,000 Jews settled in Venezuela.

Asian Immigration

In the late 1800s, people from Asia moved to the Americas. Chinese workers came to build railways in Peru and Costa Rica. People from India settled in Guyana and Suriname. People from Korea moved to Argentina, Paraguay, and Ecuador. A great many immigrants came from Japan and settled in Brazil, Bolivia, and Argentina.

People of Latin America Today

Today, most people living in Latin America are of European background. However, in Bolivia, Peru, and Ecuador, the Quechua (KECH•wah) and the Aymara (eye•mah•RAH) peoples make up most of the population. The Quechua and Aymara peoples have lived in the Andes Mountains for hundreds of years. Quechua is an official language in Bolivia and Peru.

▶ IMMIGRATION A large crowd of people eat at the Immigrants' Hotel shortly after arriving in Argentina from Europe in the early 1900s.

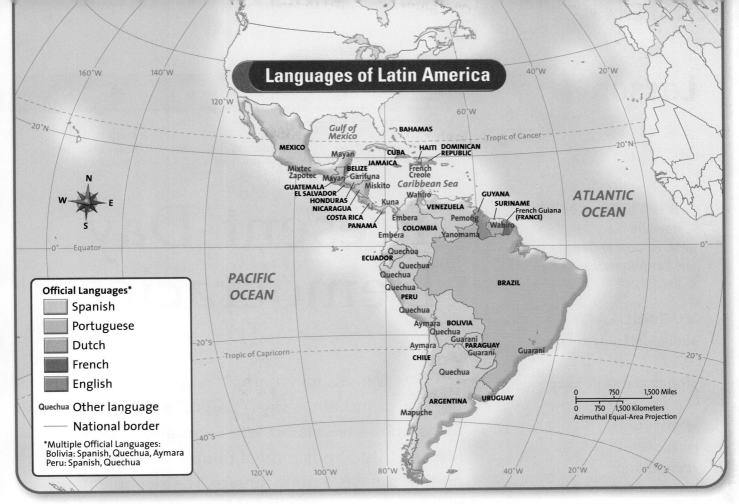

Languages of Latin America

Official Languages*
- Spanish
- Portuguese
- Dutch
- French
- English

Quechua Other language
— National border

*Multiple Official Languages:
Bolivia: Spanish, Quechua, Aymara
Peru: Spanish, Quechua

MAP SKILL **MOVEMENT** European settlement brought many European languages to Latin America. What languages are spoken in Brazil?

Most people in Central America and South America live in or near large cities. **São Paulo,** Brazil, with its surrounding area, has more than 32 million people. **Buenos Aires,** Argentina, has more than 12 million people.

Each year, the populations of urban areas in Central and South America continue to grow.

READING CHECK **SUMMARIZE**
Where did most people in Latin America come from?

REVIEW

1. WHAT TO KNOW How did Canada and Latin America grow and change in the late 1800s?

2. VOCABULARY Write a sentence describing the skills of the **vaqueros**.

3. HISTORY How did the gold rush lead to Canada's western settlement?

4. CULTURE Why did people from Europe and Asia move to Latin America in the late 1800s?

5. CRITICAL THINKING Why was the building of railroads important to Canadians?

6. WRITE A STORY Write a story about an immigrant coming to work on the Canadian Pacific Railway.

Time

1860 ———————————————— Present

1917
Mexico adopts a
new Constitution

1948
Organization of American
States is formed

1999
Nunavut becomes
a territory

WHAT TO KNOW
How did the
governments of Canada
and Latin America change
in the 1900s?

VOCABULARY
parliamentary democracy
p. 79
presidential democracy
p. 79
ejido p. 81
junta p. 83
guerrilla p. 83
Commonwealth of Nations
p. 84
bilingual p. 84
federal system p. 85
separatism p. 85

PEOPLE
Porfirio Díaz
Pancho Villa
Emiliano Zapata
Vicente Fox
Oscar Arias Sánchez
Michelle Bachelet

PLACES
Puebla
Nunavut

**COMPARE AND
CONTRAST**

Present-Day Democracies

YOU ARE THERE

"What's happening?" you ask. Your grandfather says "shush," as your mother turns up the television. It is February, 2006, in Mexico City. Thousands of people have gathered in the city's main square. Their candidate in the July presidential election is about to give a speech. There are five candidates on the ballot. Your family wants to hear what all of the candidates have to say before they decide how they will cast their votes.

> **RALLY FOR PRESIDENTIAL
CANDIDATES in Mexico City, 2006**

▶ **CANADA'S PARLIAMENT** is made up of the House of Commons and the Senate. This photograph shows the House of Commons.

Democracies in the Americas

Most countries in North America and South America now have democratic governments. As in all democracies, they have free elections, written constitutions, and courts that protect individual rights. Even so, there are important differences among the democratic governments of Canada and Latin America.

Parliamentary Democracy

The government of Canada is modeled after Britain's Parliament.

In a **parliamentary democracy**, the Parliament chooses the prime minister to lead the government. The prime minister is the head of the political party that wins the most seats in Parliament's House of Commons.

Presidential Democracy

Mexico's government is similar to that of the United States. Both countries are presidential democracies. A **presidential democracy** is a government in which the people elect the president to be the chief executive.

READING CHECK ⦚COMPARE AND CONTRAST

How is Canada's kind of government different from Mexico's?

Mexican Revolution

In the 1800s, Mexico's government changed hands many times. The changes rarely took place peacefully. In 1861, Benito Juárez was elected president of Mexico. One month later, his enemies asked the French government to help force him from office.

Cinco de Mayo

On May 5, 1862, about 30,000 French soldiers invaded Mexico and attacked the city of **Puebla**. An army of mestizos and Native Americans fought together to defeat the French.

The battle did not drive the French from the country. Even so, the Mexican people saw it as a great victory. The Mexican holiday of Cinco de Mayo, or "Fifth of May," celebrates this battle.

French Emperor

The French troops took control of Mexico. They named Maximilian, an Austrian prince, the emperor of Mexico. The Mexican people did not want to be ruled by a European leader. Benito Juárez fled to the north and put together a new army. In 1867, Juárez's army defeated the French troops. Juárez once again became president.

▶ **ON THE CINCO DE MAYO HOLIDAY,** Mexicans celebrate the victory over the French at the battle of Puebla.

▶ **MEXICAN REVOLUTION** Farmers march with Emiliano Zapata's army in 1914.

Porfirio Díaz

When Juárez died, **Porfirio Díaz** (paw•FEER•yoh DEE•ahs) came to power. Díaz ruled Mexico as a dictator for 30 years. Díaz ordered railroads built and factories expanded. He brought economic growth, but problems remained. United States companies bought large amounts of land. About a million people lost their farms.

Villa and Zapata

In 1910, poor farmers and workers called for a revolution to end Díaz's rule. They wanted Mexico to be a democracy again. **Pancho Villa** (VEE•ah) led them in northern Mexico.

Villa's army stood up against the owners of large haciendas and mines. **Emiliano Zapata** (ay•meel•YAHN•oh sah•PAH•tah) led the rebels in the south.

The Constitution of 1917

The Mexican Revolution ended in 1917 with the adoption of Mexico's present constitution. Under this constitution, the government divided large estates into smaller pieces of land called **ejidos** (ay•HEE•dohz). The ejidos were given to Mexican farmers.

READING CHECK **MAIN IDEA AND DETAILS**
Who led the Mexican Revolution?

Mexico's States

National capital

State capital

UNITED STATES

Mexicali ★

BAJA CALIFORNIA

30°N

SONORA

Hermosillo ★

CHIHUAHUA

Chihuahua ★

115°W

Rio Grande

COAHUILA

85°W

30°N

90°W

95°W

Gulf of California

BAJA CALIFORNIA SUR

25°N

SINALOA

Culiacán ★

DURANGO

Saltillo ★

NUEVO LEÓN

★ Monterrey

Gulf of Mexico

25°N

La Paz ★

Durango ★

ZACATECAS

Ciudad Victoria ★

Tropic of Cancer

PACIFIC OCEAN

Zacatecas ★

SAN LUIS POTOSÍ

TAMAULIPAS

NAYARIT

Tepic ★

1 ★

★ San Luis Potosí

Bay of Campeche

★ Mérida

YUCATÁN

20°N

Guadalajara ★

GUANAJUATO

Guanajuato ★

2 ★

HIDALGO

Pachuca ★

Campeche ★

QUINTANA ROO

Chetumal ★

20°N

110°W

JALISCO

Morelia ★

MICHOACÁN

5 ★ ⊛ 6

★ 3

Jalapa Enríquez ★

CAMPECHE

Caribbean Sea

Colima ★

COLIMA

★ 4

PUEBLA

Puebla

VERACRUZ

TABASCO

Villahermosa ★

Chilpancingo ★

GUERRERO

Oaxaca ★

OAXACA

Tuxtla Gutiérrez ★

CHIAPAS

BELIZE

0   150   300 Miles

0   150   300 Kilometers
Azimuthal Equal-Area Projection

GUATEMALA

HONDURAS

105°W

100°W

95°W

15°N

State	Capital City
1. AGUASCALIENTES.......	Aguascalientes
2. QUERÉTARO................	Querétaro
3. TLAXCALA....................	Tlaxcala
4. MORELOS....................	Cuernavaca
5. MÉXICO.......................	Toluca
6. DISTRITO FEDERAL......	Mexico City

MAP SKILL **REGIONS** Mexico has 31 political regions called states. Which states border the Rio Grande?

Mexico's Government

The Constitution of 1917 limits the president's term of office to six years. From 1929 to 2000, all of Mexico's presidents were members of a political party called the Partido Revolucionario Institucional (PRI). Then **Vicente Fox** won election as president in 2000. For the first time since 1929, Mexico was represented by a different political party.

Like the government of the United States, Mexico's government is organized into three branches. The three branches are the executive branch, the legislative branch, and the judicial branch. The legislative branch is called the General Congress. Members of the General Congress represent Mexico's 31 states, as well as its different political parties.

Mexico's General Congress has much less power than the United States Congress. The General Congress often simply approves the president's decisions.

READING CHECK ⊗ **COMPARE AND CONTRAST**
How is the organization of Mexico's government similar to that of the United States?

Central America and South America

In the early 1900s, Central America and South America saw years of violence and war. Military juntas fought over control of El Salvador. A **junta** (HOON•tah) is a small group of military leaders who take power.

In Colombia, **guerrillas**, or political fighters, took control of the government. Chile was ruled by the military dictator Augusta Pinochet (ah•GOOS•tah pee•noh•CHAYT) from 1975 to 1988.

Democratic Elections

The countries of Central America and South America are working toward true democratic governments. In 1986, **Oscar Arias Sánchez** was elected president of Costa Rica. To bring peace to Central America, Arias proposed a plan to set up free and fair elections. Guatemala, El Salvador, Honduras, and Nicaragua agreed to the plan. Arias was awarded the Nobel Peace Prize for his plan.

Michelle Bachelet (bah•cheh •LAY) was elected Chile's president in 2006. This was Chile's fourth democratic presidential election since Pinochet's rule ended.

Organization of American States

To help keep peace, almost all the nations of Latin America belong to the Organization of American States (OAS). Cuba is not a member. It has been ruled by a dictator since 1959.

The OAS encourages cooperation and the peaceful settlement of disputes. It works to promote free trade among its member nations. It also encourages the spread of democracy through free and fair elections.

READING CHECK **MAIN IDEA AND DETAILS**
How does OAS encourage the spread of democracy?

> **DEMOCRATIC ELECTIONS** In 2003, Nobel Prize winner Rigoberta Menchú Tum votes in Guatemala's presidential election.

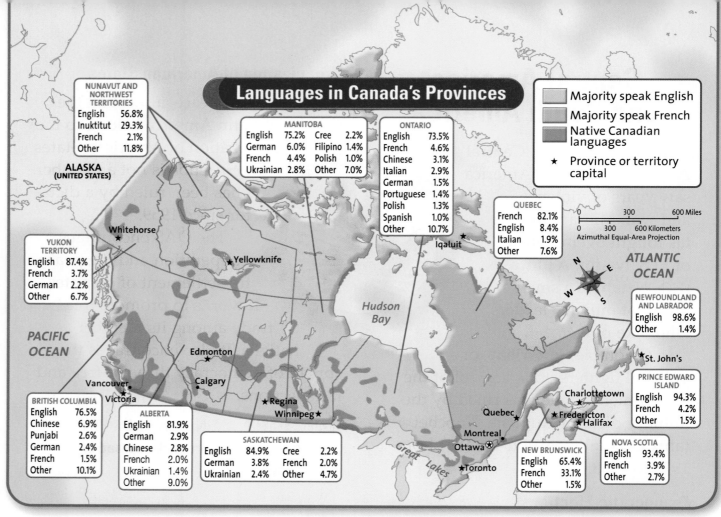

Languages in Canada's Provinces

Legend:
- Majority speak English
- Majority speak French
- Native Canadian languages
- ★ Province or territory capital

NUNAVUT AND NORTHWEST TERRITORIES
English	56.8%
Inuktitut	29.3%
French	2.1%
Other	11.8%

ALASKA (UNITED STATES)

MANITOBA
English	75.2%	Cree	2.2%
German	6.0%	Filipino	1.4%
French	4.4%	Polish	1.0%
Ukrainian	2.8%	Other	7.0%

ONTARIO
English	73.5%
French	4.6%
Chinese	3.1%
Italian	2.9%
German	1.5%
Portuguese	1.4%
Polish	1.3%
Spanish	1.0%
Other	10.7%

QUEBEC
French	82.1%
English	8.4%
Italian	1.9%
Other	7.6%

YUKON TERRITORY
English	87.4%
French	3.7%
German	2.2%
Other	6.7%

NEWFOUNDLAND AND LABRADOR
English	98.6%
Other	1.4%

PRINCE EDWARD ISLAND
English	94.3%
French	4.2%
Other	1.5%

BRITISH COLUMBIA
English	76.5%
Chinese	6.9%
Punjabi	2.6%
German	2.4%
French	1.5%
Other	10.1%

ALBERTA
English	81.9%
German	2.9%
Chinese	2.8%
French	2.0%
Ukrainian	1.4%
Other	9.0%

SASKATCHEWAN
English	84.9%	Cree	2.2%
German	3.8%	French	2.0%
Ukrainian	2.4%	Other	4.7%

NEW BRUNSWICK
English	65.4%
French	33.1%
Other	1.5%

NOVA SCOTIA
English	93.4%
French	3.9%
Other	2.7%

Cities and labels: Whitehorse, Yellowknife, Iqaluit, Hudson Bay, ATLANTIC OCEAN, PACIFIC OCEAN, St. John's, Charlottetown, Fredericton, Halifax, Quebec, Montreal, Ottawa, Toronto, Great Lakes, Edmonton, Calgary, Vancouver, Victoria, Regina, Winnipeg

0 300 600 Miles / 0 300 600 Kilometers — Azimuthal Equal-Area Projection

MAP SKILL **PLACE** Canadians speak many languages other than English, their main language. In what provinces do some people speak Ukrainian?

Canada's Government

The Constitution Act of 1982 allows Canada to change its own constitution. Canada's Parliament no longer has to ask Britain's Parliament to approve all changes. The Constitution Act also includes a Charter of Rights and Freedoms. The Charter is similar to the United States Bill of Rights.

Canada keeps its ties with Britain through its membership in the Commonwealth of Nations. The **Commonwealth of Nations** is made up mostly of those nations that were once colonies of Britain. The monarch of Britain is the head of the Commonwealth but plays mainly a symbolic role.

Bilingual Nation

In 1969, the country of Canada became a **bilingual**, or two-language, nation. English and French are Canada's two official languages. All street signs, government documents, and product labels are printed in both languages.

Not all Canadians speak English or French. Almost 100 other languages are also spoken in Canada. These languages include more than 50 Native Canadian languages.

A Federal System

Instead of 50 states, Canada has ten provinces and three territories. Even so, Canada has a federal system of government similar to the government of the United States. In a **federal system**, states or provinces share authority with the national government.

Just like the 50 states of the United States, the 10 provinces of Canada have their own legislatures. In Canada, these legislatures are called assemblies.

Separatism

The people of Quebec are proud of their French heritage. Since the 1960s, some of Quebec's people have thought about separating from Canada. **Separatism** is a movement to separate one government from another government. In 1995, the people of Quebec put the issue to a vote. The vote to separate failed.

Nunavut Territory

In 1999, **Nunavut** became Canada's newest territory. Nunavut was

> **NUNAVUT TERRITORY** An Inuit leader lights a ceremonial lamp to open the second session of Nunavut's assembly, in 2004.

created out of the eastern part of the Northwest Territories.

Most of the people who live in Nunavut are Inuit. They govern themselves by consensus, or agreement by members of the community.

READING CHECK ⏶COMPARE AND CONTRAST
How is Canada's government similar to that of Britain?

REVIEW

1. **WHAT TO KNOW** How did the governments of Canada and Latin America change in the 1900s?

2. **VOCABULARY** Use the term **parliamentary democracy** in a sentence describing Canada's national government.

3. **HISTORY** Which country has been ruled by a dictator since 1959?

4. **CIVICS AND GOVERNMENT** How is the prime minister chosen to lead Canada's government?

5. **CRITICAL THINKING** How is the role of Mexico's president different from that of the President of the United States?

6. **WRITE A SUMMARY** Write a paragraph that summarizes the similarities and differences between Canada's and Mexico's governments.

Chapter 4 ■ **85**

Canada's Economy

WHAT TO KNOW
What are the different parts of Canada's economy?

VOCABULARY
developed economy p. 87
gross domestic product p. 87
per capita income p. 87
interdependence p. 88
protectionism p. 88
free trade p. 88
market economy p. 89

PLACES
Alberta
Niagara Falls
Ontario
Toronto
Montreal
Quebec
Rideau Canal
Ottawa

COMPARE AND CONTRAST

YOU ARE THERE You and your family are visiting a farm in the province of **Alberta.** The farmer takes you on a tour of the fields. "Why are the tops of the plants bending toward the ground?" you ask. "Because the crop is ripe," the farmer answers. "We'll start harvesting next week."

On the way back to the farmer's house, you see a huge oil-drilling tower in the distance. "As soon as the oil company moved in," the farmer explains, "many of our neighbors stopped farming and started working there."

A Developed Economy

Canada has a developed economy that provides its workers with a high standard of living. A **developed economy** is one in which people use advanced technology to produce many kinds of goods and services.

Canada is one of the world's richest nations. One example of Canada's wealth is its gross domestic product, or GDP. The **gross domestic product** is the total value of goods and services that a country produces in a year. Canada's GDP amounts to more than $1 trillion.

Canada has one of the highest per capita incomes in the world. A country's **per capita income** is the amount of yearly income each person would have if the GDP were divided equally among all of the people. Canada's per capita income is about $38,400 a year. The per capita income of the United States is even higher—$45,800.

A Diverse Economy

In the early 1900s, most Canadians worked in farming, fishing, and lumber jobs. Today, about three-fourths work in service industries, such as finance, government, tourism, and recreation.

Other Canadians work in manufacturing jobs. They make wood and paper products, automobiles, chemicals, food products, or other goods.

READING CHECK ◊COMPARE AND CONTRAST
How is Canada's economy similar to that of the United States?

GRAPH Mining and agriculture are important to the economy of Alberta (below). According to the graph, what are the two most important industries in Canada?

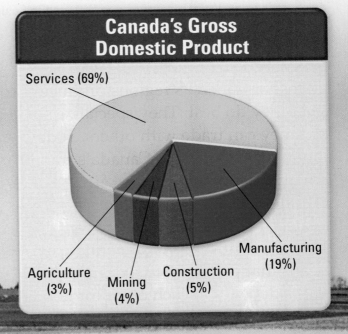

Canada's Gross Domestic Product

- Services (69%)
- Manufacturing (19%)
- Construction (5%)
- Mining (4%)
- Agriculture (3%)

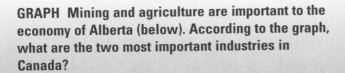

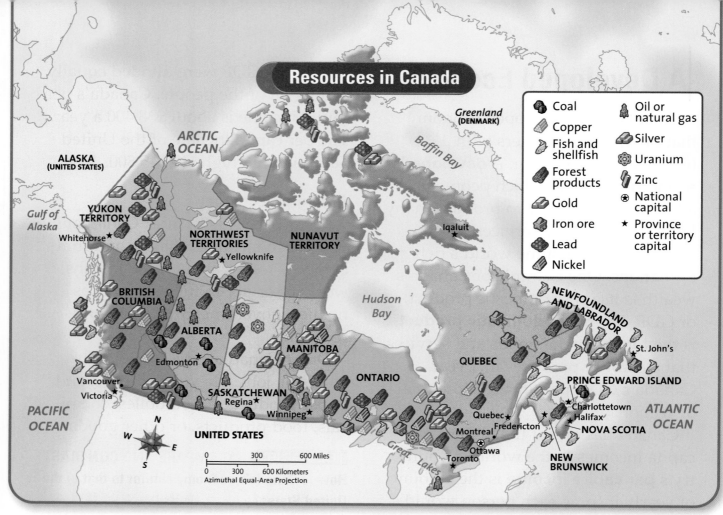

Resources in Canada

Legend			
Coal		Oil or natural gas	
Copper		Silver	
Fish and shellfish		Uranium	
Forest products		Zinc	
Gold		National capital	
Iron ore		Province or territory capital	
Lead			
Nickel			

HUMAN-ENVIRONMENT INTERACTIONS Canada has many different economic resources. What resources can be found in Saskatchewan?

A Trading Nation

Most of Canada's regions produce what they do best. They specialize so that they can trade with others. Today, about three-fourths of Canada's trade is with the United States.

Trade with the United States has created interdependence between the two countries. **Interdependence** means that people in two or more places depend on each other for goods and services.

Protectionism

For many years, Canadian leaders feared that trade with other countries would hurt their economy. In 1879, Canada set up a way to protect its businesses from outside competition. This system, known as **protectionism**, placed taxes called tariffs on products coming into Canada.

Free Trade

In the 1980s, Canada began to rethink the idea of protectionism. Businesses saw that **free trade**, or trade without tariffs, could be good for the economy. Free trade would increase the amount and kinds of goods that Canadians could buy. It would also increase the markets where Canadian goods could be sold.

In 1989, Canada and the United States entered into a free-trade agreement. In the 1990s, Mexico joined Canada and the United States. Together, they signed the North American Free Trade Agreement, or NAFTA.

NAFTA has made it easier for companies to do business with countries that signed the agreement. Many U.S. companies have opened factories in Canada. That is because salaries are lower there. However, many Canadian companies have opened factories in Mexico. There, salaries are even lower.

READING CHECK **MAIN IDEA AND DETAILS**
Which country is Canada's leading trade partner?

High-Tech Economy

Like the United States, Canada has a market economy. In a **market economy**, individuals own and control businesses. Unlike the United States, Canada's national government owns some businesses. The government provides health care to every citizen. It also supervises television stations.

The government supports the communications industry and other high-tech businesses. It even has its own space program.

READING CHECK **COMPARE AND CONTRAST**
How does Canada's market economy differ from that of the United States?

▶ **ROBERTA BONDAR** (top right) is one of at least seven Canadian astronauts who have flown on a United States space shuttle (below).

Natural Resources

Canada's water, minerals, fish, and other natural resources provide the country with much wealth. Canadians work hard to protect their country's natural resources. They try to conserve their resources and keep Canada free from pollution.

Recycling and Hydroelectricity

The Canadian government encourages its citizens to recycle used goods. It also supports the use of cheap, clean energy sources, such as hydroelectricity. Hydroelectricity is electricity made by using the power of flowing water. Canada makes the most hydroelectricity in the world.

READING CHECK **CAUSE AND EFFECT**
What steps have Canadians taken to protect their environment?

Tourism and Sports

Canada's natural resources are important to Canada's booming tourism and sports industries. Each year, thousands of tourists visit Canada to enjoy the country's beauty. They fish, sail, hike, and go mountain-biking in Canada's national parks.

Tourism

One of the most popular tourist attractions is **Niagara Falls.** Niagara Falls is located on the border between **Ontario** and the United States.

Tourists visit Canada's cities as well. **Toronto,** Canada's largest city, is home to people of many different cultures.

In the city of Montreal, tourists stroll along cobblestone streets and visit buildings that date from the 1600s. **Montreal** and **Quebec**

⚡FAST FACT

Many Canadians use the word *hydro* instead of the word *electricity*. This hydroelectric dam is in Alberta.

▶ **ICE-SKATING is an important part of everyday life along the Rideau Canal in Ottawa.**

are the centers of French-Canadian culture.

The **Rideau Canal** (rih•DOH) in **Ottawa** is known as "the world's largest skating rink." In the winter, people skate to work and to school on the frozen canal.

Sports

The sport of ice hockey is important to Canadian culture. Ice hockey was invented in Canada in 1855. Today, thousands of Canadians play ice hockey. Canada and the United States both have professional teams in the National Hockey League.

Canadians also play their own form of football. The Canadian Football League plays its games on a 110-yard field. Canadian football follows a set of rules slightly different from those of United States football.

READING CHECK **MAIN IDEA AND DETAILS**
What sports have professional leagues in Canada?

REVIEW

1. **WHAT TO KNOW** What are the different parts of Canada's economy?

2. **VOCABULARY** Use the terms **protectionism** and **free trade** to describe Canada's reasons for signing NAFTA.

3. **CIVICS AND GOVERNMENT** Who runs Canada's health-care system?

4. **ECONOMY** What industry contributes the most to Canada's GDP?

5. **CRITICAL THINKING** How does protecting Canada's resources affect its economy?

6. **WRITE A SPEECH** Choose one of Canada's provinces. Write a speech encouraging companies to trade with that province.

Economies of Latin America

WHAT TO KNOW
In what ways are Latin American economies alike and different?

VOCABULARY
developing country p. 93
middle class p. 94
maquiladora p. 95
sharecropping p. 96
boom-and-bust economy
   p. 97
deforestation p. 97

PEOPLE
Diego Rivera
Frida Kahlo

PLACES
Mexico City

COMPARE AND CONTRAST

YOU ARE THERE
You are visiting **Mexico City** with your family. As soon as you step outside the hotel, you hear loud sounds, smell strong flavors, and see bright colors. Trucks, taxis, and hand-pushed carts fight for space in the streets. The smell of freshly baked food fills the air. Your guide tells you that Mexico City is one of the largest cities in the world. It has nearly 8.6 million people.

▶ **MEXICO CITY** Many different economic activities take place in Mexico City's many different neighborhoods.

Economies of Selected Latin American Counties		
Country	GDP (in billions of U.S. dollars)	Per Capita Income (in U.S. dollars)
Brazil	1,836,000	9,700
Mexico	1,346,000	12,800
Argentina	523,700	13,300
Venezuela	334,600	12,200
Guatemala	62,530	4,700
Cuba	51,110	4,500
Costa Rica	45,770	10,300
Jamaica	20,670	7,700
Belize	2,444	7,900
St. Vincent and the Grenadines	1,042	9,800

TABLE Which country in this table has the highest GDP? Which country has the highest per capita income?

Developing Countries

Like the United States and Canada, some Latin American countries have developed economies. These countries include Mexico, Brazil, Venezuela, Chile, Uruguay, and Argentina.

Other countries in Latin America are considered developing countries. A **developing country** is one with an economy that is still being built up.

Developing countries have few resources and little technology. They do not produce many goods, and they have low per capita incomes.

Life in Developing Countries

Some experts say that countries with a per capita income below $9,200 are developing countries. Haiti, Guatemala, Bolivia, Cuba, and Guyana all have per capita incomes under $5,000. Even developed countries in Latin America do not have high per capita incomes. Mexico's is just $12,800.

READING CHECK ⵙ**COMPARE AND CONTRAST**
How do the economies of Latin America's developing countries differ from those of developed countries?

▶ **VENEZUELAN MONEY**

Mexico's Economy

For most of Mexico's history, the economy has been based on farming and mining. Yet since the 1940s, Mexico's government has worked hard to promote the growth of manufacturing. Today, about one-fourth of Mexico's jobs are in steel, oil, automobile, and other industries. Yet more than two-thirds of Mexico's workers have jobs in service industries.

The growth of the economy has allowed Mexico to spend more money building new factories, roads, and housing. The government has also taken steps to reduce pollution. In addition, it has improved health care and expanded the education system.

Wealth and Poverty

Mexico is a country of wealth and poverty. The top one-fifth of the population earns more than half of the country's yearly income. Mexico's growing middle class enjoys a standard of living similar to that of the average family in the United States. The **middle class** is the group of people between the rich and the poor.

In contrast, many of Mexico's rural farmers are very poor. Some live in villages with no electricity or running water. Most of the poorest farms are in central and southern Mexico and on the Yucatán Peninsula.

Many of the farmers in the southern region have Mayan backgrounds. They survive by growing corn, beans, and other crops in rocky soil.

❯ **A NATIVE AMERICAN WEAVER** in the rural village of Oaxaca (wah•HAH•kah) sells colorful handmade rugs in an outdoor market.

▶ **IN SILAO, MEXICO,** factory workers put together a truck in a plant owned by an American company.

City Life

Many people have moved from rural areas to Mexico's cities to find jobs. Today, about two-thirds of all Mexicans live in cities of at least 2,500 people. **Mexico City,** the largest city, has more than 8.7 million people.

People flock to Mexico City for its art, culture, sports, and festivals. Paintings by artists such as **Diego Rivera** and **Frida Kahlo** can be seen in the city's many galleries and museums.

New houses cannot be built fast enough to keep up with the growing population. Roads are jammed with traffic.

Maquiladoras

Each year, thousands of Mexicans move to border cities along the Rio Grande and in Baja California. There, American companies have built factories. Many are assembly plants known as maquiladoras (mah•kee•lah•DOH•rahs). In a **maquiladora**, workers put together products from parts made by other companies. The finished products are shipped to stores in the United States.

Immigration to the United States

Many poor Mexicans are attracted by promises of a better life in the United States. Each year, millions of Mexicans enter the United States illegally. Illegal immigrants are those without the needed papers to enter a country. Mexico and the United States are working to find solutions to illegal immigration.

READING CHECK ☷COMPARE AND CONTRAST
How has Mexico's economy changed since the 1940s?

Economic Resources of Latin America

Natural Resources
- △ Bauxite
- ◇ Copper
- 🐟 Fish and shellfish
- 🪵 Forest products
- 💎 Gemstones
- ⛏ Gold
- ◆ Iron ore
- ◼ Lead
- 🛢 Oil
- ⬦ Silver
- ◊ Tin
- ◊ Zinc

Agricultural Products
- 🍌 Bananas
- 🫘 Beans
- 🌶 Cacao
- 🐂 Cattle
- ☕ Coffee
- 🌽 Corn
- ❀ Cotton
- 🌾 Grains
- 🍊 Oranges
- 🐑 Sheep
- 🌱 Sugarcane
- 🍂 Tobacco

MAP SKILL HUMAN–ENVIRONMENT INTERACTIONS What resources are the people of Bolivia likely to make use of?

Central America and South America

For many years, Central and South American countries exported mainly raw materials. People in other countries bought raw materials to manufacture products. They then sold those products for a high profit.

Today, more and more countries are using their resources to manufacture products themselves. That way, they earn more money.

Argentina, Chile, and Brazil are leading manufacturing countries. Venezuela has become a major oil producer. Most other countries rely on farming and mining.

Cash Crops

Countries such as Argentina and Brazil have some of the largest farms in the world. Sharecroppers do much of the work on these farms. In a **sharecropping** system, a landowner gives a worker shelter, tools, and seeds to farm the land. At harvest-time, the landowner takes part of the crop as payment.

Large commercial farms across Central and South America produce cash crops for export. Cash crops are crops that people raise to sell rather

DEFORESTATION Scientists use satellite images (right) and computer programs to measure how fast the Amazon rain forest (above) is shrinking.

than to use themselves. Often, landowners try to use as much of their land as possible for cash-crop farming. Guatemala's main cash crops are coffee and bananas.

In many countries, there is not enough farmland left to grow food to feed the people. Countries that depend on cash crops experience boom-and-bust economies. A **boom-and-bust economy** is one that does well for a time and suddenly weakens.

Rain Forests

In Brazil, thousands of acres of the Amazon rain forest have been cleared. The clearing of the land for farming and roads is called **deforestation**. As the Amazon rain forest shrinks, many animals face extinction. Organizations in Brazil and around the world are working to protect the Amazon rain forest.

READING CHECK **COMPARE AND CONTRAST**
How is Guatemala's economy similar to the economy of Argentina?

REVIEW

1. **WHAT TO KNOW** In what ways are Latin American economies alike and different?
2. **VOCABULARY** Write a sentence about the growth of Mexico's economy, using the word **maquiladora**.
3. **ECONOMY** What kind of resource helped Venezuela develop its economy?
4. **CULTURE** What challenges face the people living in Mexico City?
5. **CRITICAL THINKING** How do you think the economies of Latin America compare to the economy of Canada?
6. **MAKE A CHART** Make a chart using the Almanac on pages R5—R6. Include the crops and manufactured goods of the Central American countries.

Review and Test Prep

 Vocabulary

Identify the term from the word bank that correctly matches each definition.

1. farmers trade part of their crops to a land-owner for shelter, tools, and seeds

2. an economy that does well for a while and then suddenly weakens

3. people in two or more places depend on each other for goods and services

4. the total value of goods and services that a country produces in a year

5. the Royal Canadian Mounted Police

6. a group of military leaders who take power

7. a small farm resulting from the government dividing up large estates

8. provinces or states share power with the national government

Word Bank

Mounties p. 74 **gross domestic product** p. 87

ejido p. 81 **interdependence** p. 88

junta p. 83 **sharecropping** p. 96

federal system p. 85 **boom-and-bust economy** p. 97

 Facts and Main Ideas

Answer these questions.

9. What are the main Latin American countries where British and Dutch settled?

10. What kind of government has free elections, a written constitution, and individual rights?

11. What are some examples of service industries?

12. What kind of economies do Mexico, Brazil, Venezuela, and Uruguay have?

Write the letter of the best choice.

13. Which part of Canada had a gold rush in the 1890s?
    A British Columbia
    B Manitoba
    C the Klondike
    D Quebec

14. Who ruled Mexico between 1929 and 2000?
    A the PRI
    B a dictator
    C Canada
    D the judicial branch

15. What does "per capita income" mean?
    A the income of the richest people
    B the average income of those who work
    C the gross domestic product divided by the population
    D the gross domestic product divided by the average income

 Critical Thinking

16. How do tariffs on imported products protect a country's industries?

17. Why do you think that almost 100 languages are spoken in Canada?

writing

Write a Speech Imagine that you are the leader of a Latin American country. You are invited to give a speech at a meeting of the Organization of American States. Write a speech about the importance of having democratic elections.

Canada

R1

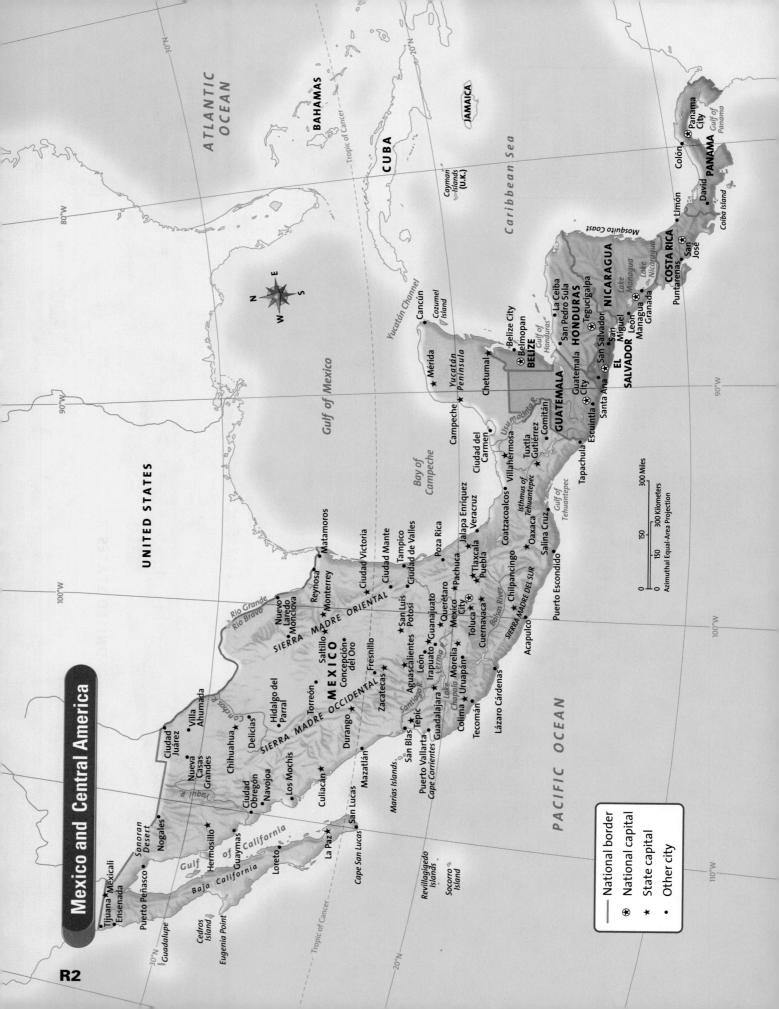

Mexico and Central America

UNITED STATES

ATLANTIC OCEAN

BAHAMAS

Tropic of Cancer

CUBA

JAMAICA

Cayman Islands (U.K.)

Caribbean Sea

Gulf of Mexico

Bay of Campeche

Yucatán Channel

Cancún
Cozumel Island

Mérida
Yucatán Peninsula

Campeche

Ciudad del Carmen

Chetumal

Belize City
Belmopan ⊛
BELIZE
Gulf of Honduras

La Ceiba
San Pedro Sula

HONDURAS
Tegucigalpa ⊛
Mosquito Coast

NICARAGUA

Lake Managua
Managua ⊛
León
Granada
Lake Nicaragua

COSTA RICA
Puntarenas
San José ⊛
Limón

PANAMA
David
Colón
Panama City ⊛
Gulf of Panama
Coiba Island

Villahermosa
Tuxtla Gutiérrez
Comitán
Usumacinta R.

GUATEMALA
Guatemala City ⊛
Escuintla
Santa Ana
San Salvador ⊛
EL SALVADOR
San Miguel

Tapachula

Coatzacoalcos
Isthmus of Tehuantepec
Salina Cruz
Gulf of Tehuantepec

Oaxaca
Veracruz
Jalapa Enríquez
Poza Rica
Tampico
Ciudad de Valles
Ciudad Mante
Ciudad Victoria
Matamoros
Reynosa
Monterrey

Tlaxcala
Puebla
Pachuca
Querétaro
Mexico City ⊛
Toluca
Cuernavaca
Chilpancingo
Acapulco
Puerto Escondido
Lázaro Cárdenas

SIERRA MADRE DEL SUR

Morelia
Colima
Uruapán
Tecomán

MEXICO

Guadalajara
Tepic
Guanajuato
León
Irapuato
Aguascalientes
San Luis Potosí
Zacatecas
Fresnillo
Concepción del Oro
Saltillo
Monclova
Nuevo Laredo

SIERRA MADRE ORIENTAL

Rio Grande
Rio Bravo

Durango
Torreón
Hidalgo del Parral
Delicias
Chihuahua
Ciudad Juárez
Nueva Casas Grandes
Villa Ahumada

SIERRA MADRE OCCIDENTAL

Conchos R.
Yaqui R.

San Blas
Puerto Vallarta
Cape Corrientes
Mazatlán
Culiacán
Los Mochis
Ciudad Obregón
Navojoa
Guaymas
Hermosillo
Nogales
Puerto Peñasco
Sonoran Desert
Mexicali
Tijuana
Ensenada

Lake Chapala
Lerma R.
Santiago R.
Bolsos R.

Marías Islands
Revillagigedo Islands
Socorro Island

Baja California
Gulf of California
La Paz
Loreto
San Lucas
Cape San Lucas

Cedros Island
Eugenia Point
Guadalupe

PACIFIC OCEAN

Tropic of Cancer

300 Miles
300 Kilometers
150
0
Azimuthal Equal-Area Projection

Legend:
— National border
⊛ National capital
★ State capital
• Other city

R2

Caribbean Islands

ATLANTIC OCEAN

Gulf of Mexico

Tropic of Cancer

UNITED STATES

Straits of Florida

BAHAMAS

Grand Bahama
Freeport

Great Abaco

Eleuthera

Nassau
New Providence

Cat Island

San Salvador

Andros Island

Long Island

Great Exuma

Crooked Island

Acklins Island

Mayaguana

Turks and Caicos Islands (U.K.)

Pinar del Río
Havana
Matanzas
Nueva Gerona
Santa Clara
Cienfuegos
Cape San Antonio
Isla de la Juventud
CUBA
Camagüey
Victoria de las Tunas
Manzanillo
Holguín
Bayamo
Santiago de Cuba
Guantánamo

Cayman Islands (U.K.)
George Town
Grand Cayman

Montego Bay
Kingston
JAMAICA

W E S T

Great Inagua

Windward Passage

Cap-Haïtien
Gonaïves
HAITI
Port-au-Prince

Cape Falso

I N D I E S

Santiago
DOMINICAN REPUBLIC
Hispaniola
San Pedro de Macoris
Santo Domingo

Cape Beata

G r e a t e r

A n t i l l e s

Mona Passage

Puerto Rico (U.S.)
San Juan
Mayagüez
Ponce

St. Croix

Virgin Islands (U.S. and U.K.)

Anguilla (U.K.)
St. Martin (FRANCE and NETHERLANDS)
St. Barthélemy (FRANCE)
Basseterre
ST. KITTS AND NEVIS
Barbuda
St. John's
Antigua
ANTIGUA AND BARBUDA
Montserrat (U.K.)

Guadeloupe (FRANCE)
Pointe-à-Pitre

DOMINICA
Roseau

Martinique (FRANCE)
Fort-de-France

Castries
ST. LUCIA

BARBADOS
Bridgetown

Kingstown
ST. VINCENT AND THE GRENADINES

GRENADA
St. George's

Tobago
TRINIDAD AND TOBAGO
Port-of-Spain
Trinidad

Leeward Islands

Windward Islands

L e s s e r   A n t i l l e s

L e s s e r   A n t i l l e s

Margarita Island (VENEZUELA)

Tortuga Island (VENEZUELA)

Netherlands Antilles (NETHERLANDS)
Bonaire
Curaçao
Willemstad

Aruba (NETHERLANDS)
Oranjestad

C a r i b b e a n   S e a

VENEZUELA

COLOMBIA

HONDURAS

NICARAGUA

N E S W

Legend
— National border
⊛ National capital
• Other city

200 Miles
200 Kilometers
Lambert Conformal Conic Projection
0   100   200
0   100

R3

South America

Almanac
Facts About the Americas

Country Flag	Country	Population	Area (sq. mi.)	Capital	Economy
North America					
	Antigua and Barbuda	68,722	171	St. John's	tourism, manufacturing, construction
	Bahamas	301,790	5,386	Nassau	tourism, banking, pharmaceuticals, fishing
	Barbados	279,254	166	Bridgetown	sugar, tourism, manufacturing
	Belize	279,457	8,867	Belmopan	sugar, bananas, clothing products, tourism
	Canada	33,098,932	3,851,809	Ottowa	nickel, zinc, copper, gold, livestock, fish, chemicals, wood and paper products, petroleum
	Costa Rica	4,016,173	19,730	San José	furniture, aluminum, textiles, fertilizer, bananas, coffee, construction materials
	Cuba	11,346,670	42,803	Havana	food processing, tobacco, sugar, rice, coffee, cobalt, nickel, iron, copper, salt, textiles
	Dominica	69,029	289	Roseau	tourism, bananas, citrus fruits, pumice, soap, furniture, cement blocks
	Dominican Republic	8,950,034	18,815	Santo Domingo	cement, tourism, sugar, cocoa, coffee, nickel, bauxite, gold
	El Salvador	6,704,932	8,124	San Salvador	food products, tobacco, coffee, corn, sugar, chemicals, fertilizer, textiles
	Grenada	89,502	131	St. George's	textiles, spices, bananas, cocoa, tourism, construction
	Guatemala	14,655,189	42,042	Guatemala City	furniture, rubber, textiles, coffee, sugar, bananas, oil and petroleum, chemicals, metals
	Haiti	8,121,622	10,714	Port-au-Prince	textiles, coffee, sugar, bananas, bauxite, tourism, cement
	Honduras	6,975,204	43,277	Tegucigalpa	textiles, wood products, bananas, sugar, gold, silver, copper, lead
	Jamaica	2,731,832	4,243	Kingston	tourism, sugar, coffee, bananas, potatoes, bauxite, limestone, textiles
	Mexico	106,202,903	761,602	Mexico City	steel, chemicals, textiles, rubber, petroleum, tourism, cotton, coffee, automobiles
	Nicaragua	5,465,100	49,998	Managua	food processing, chemicals, textiles, cotton, fruits, coffee, gold, silver, copper

Country Flag	Country	Population	Area (sq. mi.)	Capital	Economy
	Panama	3,039,150	30,193	Panama City	oil refining, international banking, bananas, rice, copper, mahogany, shrimp, cement
	St. Kitts–Nevis	38,958	96	Basseterre	sugar, tourism, cotton, salt, clothing, footwear
	St. Lucia	166,312	238	Castries	clothing, tourism, bananas, coconuts, beverages, wood products
	St. Vincent and the Grenadines	117,534	150	Kingstown	tourism, bananas, arrowroot, coconuts, food processing, clothing, furniture
	Trinidad and Tobago	1,088,644	1,980	Port of Spain	oil and natural gas, chemicals, tourism, sugar, cocoa, asphalt, cotton textiles
	United States of America	295,734,134	3,537,441	Washington, D.C.	wheat, corn, coal, lead, uranium, iron, copper, gold, computers, electronics

South America

Country Flag	Country	Population	Area (sq. mi.)	Capital	Economy
	Argentina	39,537,943	1,068,296	Buenos Aires	food processing, automobiles, chemicals, grains, oil, lead, textiles, printing, steel
	Bolivia	8,857,870	424,162	La Paz/Sucre	mining, tobacco, coffee, sugar, potatoes, soybeans, tin, tungsten, handicrafts, clothing
	Brazil	186,112,794	3,286,470	Brasília	steel, automobiles, textiles, coffee, soybeans, sugar, iron, manganese, shoes, chemicals
	Chile	15,980,912	292,257	Santiago	fish, wood, grains, grapes, beans, copper, cement, textiles
	Colombia	42,954,279	439,735	Bogotá	textiles, food processing, coffee, rice, bananas, emeralds, oil, gas, cement
	Ecuador	13,363,593	109,483	Quito	food processing, bananas, coffee, oil, gas, copper, zinc, silver, gold, textiles
	Guyana	765,283	83,000	Georgetown	mining, textiles, sugar, bauxite, diamonds, gold, rice, fishing
	Paraguay	6,347,884	157,043	Asunción	food processing, textiles, cement, corn, cotton, iron, manganese, limestone, sugar
	Peru	27,925,628	496,222	Lima	fishing, mining, textiles, cotton, sugar, coffee, rice, copper, silver, gold, oil, auto assembly
	Suriname	439,117	63,039	Paramaribo	aluminum, food processing, rice, sugar, fruits, bauxite, iron, fishing
	Uruguay	3,431,932	68,039	Montevideo	meatpacking, textiles, fishing, corn, wheat, oil refining, food processing, chemicals
	Venezuela	25,375,281	352,143	Caracas	steel, textiles, coffee, rice, corn, oil, gas, iron, petroleum, mining

Glossary

The Glossary contains important history and social science words and their definitions, listed in alphabetical order. Each word is respelled as it would be in a dictionary. When you see this mark ´ after a syllable, pronounce that syllable with more force. The page number at the end of the definition tells where the word is first used in this book.

add, āce, câre, pälm; end, ēqual; it, īce; odd, ōpen, ôrder; tŏŏk, pōōl; up, bûrn; yōō as *u* in *fuse;* oil; pout; ə as *a* in *above, e* in *sicken, i* in *possible, o* in *melon, u* in *circus;* **ch**eck; ri**ng**; **th**in; **th**is; **zh** as in *vision*

Acadian (ə•kā´dē•ən) A French-speaking person who lived in British-controlled Nova Scotia. p. 39

Act of Union (akt əv yōōn´yən) An 1840 law that combined Upper and Lower Canada into the United Province of Canada. p. 64

agriculture (a´gri•kəl•chər) Farming. p. 20

alliance (ə•lī´əns) Formal partnership among groups or individuals. p. 35

altiplano (al•ti•plä´nō) High plain. p. 17

bilingual (bī•ling´gwel) Having two official languages. p. 84

boom-and-bust economy (boom ənd bust i•kä´nə•mē) An economy that does well for a time and suddenly weakens. p. 97

British North America Act (bri´tish nôrth ə•mer´ə•kə akt) An 1867 law that united all of Canada into one nation called the Dominion of Canada. p. 64

Canadian Pacific Railway A railroad in Canada that stretched from Victoria, British Columbia, to Montreal, Quebec. p. 73

civilization (si•və•lə•zā´shən) A group of people with its own ways of life, religion, and learning. p. 22

colony (kä´lə•nē) A settlement ruled by another country. p. 35

Commonwealth of Nations (kä´mən•welth əv nā´shənz) Group of nations that were once colonies of Britain. p. 84

Comunero Rebellion (kə•myōō•ne´rō ri•bel´yən) An uprising against Spanish taxes in 1780 in the Viceroyalty of New Granada. p. 55

confederation (kən•fe•də•rā´shən) A loose group of governments working together. p. 51

conquistador (kän•kēs´tə•dôr) Any of the Spanish conquerors in the Americas during the early 1500s. p. 30

Constitutional Act (kän•stə•tōō´ shə•nəl akt) A 1791 law that divided Quebec into the two provinces of Upper Canada and Lower Canada. p. 58

cordillera (kôr•dəl•yer´ə) A group of parallel mountain ranges. p. 8

coureurs de bois (kû•rûrz də bwä´) French trappers who went into Native Canadian lands in Canada to trade furs. p. 36

creole (krē´ōl) A person born to Spanish parents in Spanish America. p. 42

culture (kul´chər) A way of life shared by a group. p. 21.

deforestation (dē•fôr•ə•stā´•shən) Cutting down of most or all of the trees in an area. p. 97

developed economy (di•ve´ləpt i•kä´nə•mē) An economy in which people use advanced technology to produce many kinds of goods and services. p. 87

developing country (di•ve´lə•ping kun´trē) Country with an economy that is still being built up. p. 93

dictator (dik´tā•tər) A leader who has complete control over a government. p. 65

dominion (də•mi´nyən) A colony that has its own independent government. p. 64

ejido (ā•hē´dō) An individual farm created by dividing up large estates into smaller parts. p. 81

El Camino Real (el kä•mē´nō rā•äl´) Road system built through Mexico. p. 44.

empire (em´pīr) A collection of lands ruled by the nation that conquered them. p. 23

federal system (fe´də•rəl sis´təm) A system of government in which the power to govern is shared by the national and state governments. p. 85

First Nations (fûrst nā´shənz) Native Canadian groups in Canada. p. 19

fjord (fē•ôrd´) Narrow inlets of sea with steep cliffs. p. 7

free trade (frē trād) Trade without tariffs. p. 88

Gadsden Purchase (gadz´dən pur´chəs) Strip of land between the Colorado River and the Rio Grande bought by the United States from Mexico in 1853. p. 66

glacier (glā´shər) A large ice mass that moves slowly across land. p. 6

gold rush (gōld rush) A sudden rush of people to an area where gold has been found. p. 73

gross domestic product (grōs də•mes´tik prä´dukt) The total value of goods and services that a country produces in a year. p. 87

guerrilla (gə•ri´lə) A political fighter who takes control of a government. p. 83

hacienda (hä•sē•en´də) A large estate or home where cattle and sheep are raised. p. 43

interdependence (in•tər•də•pən´dəns) A situation in which groups of people rely on each other for goods and services. p. 88

isthmus (is´məs) A narrow strip of land that connects two areas of land. p. 12

junta (hŏŏn´tə) A group of military leaders who take control of the government. p. 83

line of demarcation (līn əv dē•mär•kā´shən) Imaginary line drawn on a map dividing lands in the Americas claimed by Spain and Portugal. p. 30

maize (māz) Kind of corn grown by early peoples in the Americas. p. 20

maquiladora (mə•kē•lə•dōr´ə) Mexican factory where workers put together products from parts made by other companies. The finished products are shipped to the United States. p. 95

market economy (mär´kət i•kä´nə•mē) An economy in which individuals own and control businesses. p. 89

mestizo (me•stē´zō) A person with both Spanish and Native American backgrounds. p. 42

Métis (mā•tēs´) Canadian of French and Native Canadian backgrounds. p. 36

middle class (mi´dəl klas) The group of people between the rich and the poor. p. 94

mission (mi´shən) A religious settlement. p. 44

missionary (mi´shə•ner•ē) A religious teacher sent out by a church to spread its religion. p. 37

Mounties (moun´tēz) Another name for the Royal Canadian Mounted Police. p. 74

mulatto (mə•la´tō) A person with both African and European backgrounds. p. 42

muskeg (mus´keg) Boggy swampland. p. 7

navigation (na•və•gā´shən) The science of planning and following a route. p. 29

Northwest Passage (nôrth´west• pasij) A waterway in North America thought to connect the Atlantic Ocean and the Pacific Ocean. p. 32

parliamentary democracy (pär•lə•men´tə•rē di•mä´krə•sē) A democracy in which the Parliament chooses the prime minister to lead the government. p. 79

peninsula (pə•nin´sə•lə) A piece of land that is mostly surrounded by water. p. 13

peninsular (pā•nēn•soo•lär) Someone in Latin America born in Spain or Portugal. p. 42.

per capita income (pər ka´pə•tə in´kəm) The amount of yearly income each person in a country would have if the GDP were divided equally among everybody. p. 87

permafrost (pûr´mə•frôst) Thin layer of frozen soil. p. 6

Plan of Iguala (plan əv i•gwä´lə) Plan that made Mexico an independent empire. p. 61

presidential democracy (pre•zə•den´shəl di•mä´krə•sē) A government in which the people elect the president to be the chief executive. p. 79

presidio (pri•sē´dē•ō) A Spanish fort. p. 44.

prime minister (prīm mi´nə•stər) Chief executive of a parliamentary democracy. p. 64

protectionism (prə•tek´shə•ni•zəm) A system of placing taxes called tariffs on products coming into a country. p. 88

Quebec Act (kwi•bek´ akt) A 1774 law that allowed French Canadians to keep their own religion and language. p. 53

rain forest (rān fôr´əst) A woodland that gets a large amount of rainfall. p. 16

Red River Settlement (red ri´vər sə´tel•ment) The first Canadian settlement northwest of Lake Superior. p 59

republic (ri•pu´blik) A form of government in which people elect representatives to run the government. p. 61

Ring of Fire (ring əv fīr) A circle of volcanoes along the edges of the Pacific Ocean. p. 14

seigneur (sān•yər´) A wealthy person who rented land to farmers. p. 37

self-sufficient (self•sə•fi´shənt) Able to provide for one's own needs without help. p. 43

separatism (se´pə•rə•ti•zəm) Belief that one's province should become an independent nation p. 85

sharecropping (shâr´krä•ping) A system of working the land in which the landowner takes part of the crops as payment. p. 96

sierra (sē•er´ə) Rugged chain of mountains. p. 13

slavery (slā´və•rē) The practice of holding people against their will and making them work without pay. p. 43

tide (tīd) The regular rise and fall of the ocean and bodies of water connected to it. p. 8

timberline (tim´bər•līn) Tree line. p. 6

trade winds (trād windz) Wind blowing consistently from the northeast and southeast toward the equator. p. 15

tributary A river or stream that flows into a larger river or stream. p. 16

triangular trade (trī•ang´gyə•lər trād) Shipping routes that connected England, the English colonies, and Africa. p. 43

tundra (tun´drə) A cold, dry region where trees cannot grow. p. 6

United Empire Loyalist (yoo•nī´təd em´pīr loi´ə•list) American colonists who remained loyal to Britain during the American Revolution. p. 57

vaquero (vä•ker´ō) Mexican cowhand. p. 75

viceroyalty (vīs´roi•əl•tē) Colony led by a viceroy appointed by the king. p. 41

voyageur (voi•ə•zhûr´) A trapper who traveled the rivers and lakes in search of furs. p. 36

Index

PHOTOGRAPH CREDITS

Page Placement Key: (t) top; **(b)** bottom; **(c)** center; **(l)** left; **(r)** right; **(bg)** background; **(i)** insert.

Table of Contents: iii (bg) John Shaw/ Panoramic Images/NGSImages.com, (l) Michael J.P. Scott/Getty Images, (r) based on Theophile Hamel, *Samuel de Champlain,* oil on canvas, courtesy of Collection of the Governor General of Canada, Le Citadelle, Quebec, Library and Archives Canada, Accession # 1997-476-73; iv (l) Photographs and Prints Division/Schomberg Center for Research in Black Culture/New York Public Library/Astor, Lenox and Tilden Foundations, (b) Corbis, (r) Larry Luxner/ ddbstock.

Chapter 1: 1 (bg) Jeremy Woodhouse/Getty Images, (bl) John Shaw/Panoramic Images/ NGSImages.com, (bc) Bruce Dale/National Geographic Image Collection; 4 Janet Foster/ Masterfile; 6 (i) William A. Bake/Corbis, (b) Stuart A. McCall/Mira; 8-9 John Shaw/ Panoramic Images/NGSImages.com; 9 (tr) Richard T. Nowitz/Corbis; 10-11 Don Couch Photography; 12 (i) Bruce Dale/National Geographic Image Collection, 12-13 Randy Faris/Corbis; 13 (t) Oleg Cajko/Panoramic Images; 14 Jeff Greenberg/eStock Photo; 15 Corbis; 17 Frans Lemmens/Getty Images; 23 Michael J.P. Scott/Getty Images.

Chapter 2: 25 (bg) Wolfgang Kaehler/ Corbis, (bl) Gordon Miller, (br) Archivo Iconografico, S.A./Corbis; 28 National Geographic Magazine/UCLA Museum of Cultural History; 29 Wolfgang Kaehler/ Corbis; 30 (i) Canadian Museum of Civilization, (b) Gordon Miller; 32 Gordon Miller; 33 Marc-Aurele de Foy Suzor-

Cote, *Jacque Cartier Meeting the Indians at Stadacona, 1535,* oil on canvas, 266x401cm, Collection: Musee national des beaux-arts du Quebec, Accession # 34.12, photographer Jean-Guy Kerouac; 35 Theophile Hamel, *Samuel de Champlain,* oil on canvas, courtesy of Collection of the Governor General of Canada, Le Citadelle, Quebec, Library and Archives Canada, Accession # 1997-476-73; 36 Richard Short, detail of *A View of the Intendants' Palace* (Quebec, Quebec), Library and Archives Canada, Accession # C-000360; 38 Lowell Georgia/Corbis; 39 Laurie Platt Winfrey/The Art Archive; 42 (b) Archivo Iconografico, S.A./Corbis, (i) Courtesy of Museum of Textil y de la indiumen-taria; Ramon Manent/CORBIS; 44 John Elk Photography; 45 The Granger Collection, New York.

Chapter 3: 47 (bg) Jose Fuste Raga/ageFo-tostock, (bl) University of Moncton , (br) Corbis; 52 (tl) Don Troiani/Military and Historical Image Bank, (tr) Edward Penny, *The Death of General Wolfe,* oil on can-vas, 102x127 cm, WA 1845.38, Ashmolean Museum of Art and Archaeology; 53 George Craig, *The Deportation of Acadians,* 1893, University of Moncton; 54 Peruvian Colonial Reales, 1760, Fourobert.8921, 1966.16.4, Archives, American Numismatic Society; 55 The Art Archive/Rodriguez Figueroa col-lection, Lima/Mirelle Vautier; 58 (b) Corbis, (i) National Gallery of Canada/Canadian War Museum; 59 James B. Dennis, Battle of Queenston Heights, oil on canvas, 54.4x76.3 cm, 24596, Thomas Moore Photography/ ©Weir Foundation; 60 (tr) Photographs and Prints Division/Schomberg Center for Research in Black Culture/New York Public Library/Astor, Lenox and Tilden Foundations, (bl) *Simon Bolivar* (1783-1801),

oil on canvas by Lovera, Juan (1776-1841) ©Atwater Kent Museum of Philadelphia/ The Bridgeman Art Library; 61 Archivo Iconografico, S.A./Corbis; 64 Corbis; 66 The Granger Collection, New York; 67 Museo Nacional de Bellas Artes Buenos Aires/Dagli Orti/The Art Archive.

Chapter 4: 69 (bg) Donald Nausman/ Getty Images, (bl) Bettmann/Corbis, (bc) CPimages/Canadian Press, (br) Danny Lehman/Corbis; 72 Bettmann/Corbis; 74 (tr) Scala/Art Resource; 74 (bl) Paul A. Souders/ Corbis; 75 *Vaqueros Roping Steer,* Charles Christian Nahls, oil on canvas, Courtesy of Anschutz Collection; 76 Library of Congress; 78 Alfredo Estrella/AFP/Getty Images; 79 The Canadian Press/Tom Hanson; 80 (b) Ziegler/The Image Finders, (i) The Granger Collection; 81 Corbis; 83 (t) Organization of American States, (br) Associated Press, PRENSA Photographer Edwin Castro; 85 CPimages/Canadian Press; 86-87 Pics Inc./ Alamy; 89 Canadian Space Agency Image Gallery; 90 Gordon Petersen/FirstLight; 91 John Sylvester/Alamy; 92 Don Couch Photography; 93 Larry Luxner/ddbstock; 94 Russell Gordon/Odyssey Productions, Inc.; 95 Danny Lehman/Corbis; 97 (i) NASA Visible Earth Catalog, (t) Smith, Nigel J.H./ Animals Animals-Earth Scenes.

All other photos © Houghton Mifflin Harcourt School Publishers. Houghton Mifflin Harcourt Photos provided by the Houghton Mifflin Harcourt Index : Houghton Mifflin Harcourt IPR : and Houghton Mifflin Harcourt photographers; Weronica Ankarorn : Victoria Bowen : Eric Camden : Doug Dukane : Ken Kinzie : April Riehm : and Steve Williams.

HOUGHTON
MIFFLIN
HARCOURT
School Publishers

ISBN-13: 978-0-153-85889-5

9 780153 858895

1180521